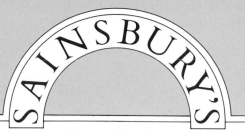

SAINSBURY'S
HEALTHY·EATING
·COOKBOOKS·

Raw Food

SARAH BROWN

CONTENTS

INTRODUCTION 5–8

INGREDIENTS 9–20

STARTERS
Soups 21–24 • Dips 26–33 • Relishes 34

MAIN COURSES
Stuffed vegetables 35–40 • Loaves and rissoles 41–43
Chunky salads 43–50 • Coleslaws 50–54 • Leaf and sprout salads 54–61
Root, shoot and fruit salads 61–66 • Salad dressings 66–74

DESSERTS
Fruit and nut desserts 75, 81–2 • Fruit salads 76–78
Dried fruits 79

FRUIT JUICES AND SNACKS
Fruit juices 84–86 • Snacks 87–89

NUTRITION CHARTS 90–93

Raw Food was conceived, edited and designed by Dorling Kindersley Limited, 9 Henrietta Street, London WC2E 8PS

Published exclusively for J Sainsbury plc, Stamford House, Stamford Street, London SE1 9LL
by Dorling Kindersley Limited, 9 Henrietta Street, London WC2E 8PS

First published 1986

Copyright © 1986 by Dorling Kindersley Limited, London   Text copyright © 1986 by Sarah Elizabeth Brown Limited

ISBN 0-86318-144-9

Printed in Italy

INTRODUCTION

*Raw food conjures up images of endless plates of carrots and lettuce leaves.
But this is far from the truth, because an astonishing number of ingredients
can be eaten raw and combined in any number of ways – from roots,
shoots and fruits, to cereals, nuts, seeds and spices, and a wide range of
dairy products and unusual alternatives.*

WHAT IS THE APPEAL OF RAW FOOD?

You only need to walk through the fruit and vegetable section of a supermarket to appreciate the vibrant colour combinations of fresh food, and when served uncooked it loses none of its appeal. Raw food also offers a wide variety of textures – not only crunchy salads and savouries, but grainy dips and pâtés, chewy loaves and rissoles, velvety creams and dressings, and smooth drinks and relishes. But more important than colour and texture is convenience. Preparing raw food is quick, easy and inexpensive. With basic equipment, you can concoct light or substantial meals within minutes, without ever turning on the oven.

WHY RAW FOOD IS GOOD FOR YOU

Eating some foods raw is an essential part of a healthy diet. It can help to keep your weight down, it increases your sense of vitality and wellbeing, and can build up resistance to some diseases and fatigue.

A diet high in raw fruit and vegetables is naturally high in fibre. This makes you feel full, and so helps prevent overeating, cleanses the body of stored wastes and toxins and aids the functioning of the digestive system. It also reduces the amount of fat absorbed by the digestive system.

By relying on fresh, uncooked produce, you will not only avoid the additives contained in processed foods, but also ensure that none of the natural essential nutrients have been lost in cooking or preserving. The B Vitamins, Vitamin C and E are water-soluble and can be lost both in preparation and cooking in water. The Vitamin C content also deteriorates with storage, Vitamin B_2 is destroyed by light, and many nutrients which lie just under the skin of vegetables and fruit are lost by peeling. Fats and proteins are both sensitive to heat.

A balance of raw and cooked food is ideal. You will enjoy many of the benefits of raw food by initially using the recipes in this book alongside your normal diet, but it is worth gradually changing the balance until you are eating more raw than cooked food.

WHAT IS A HEALTHY DIET?

There now seems little question that good health is dependent on a healthy diet, no smoking and plenty of exercise. But what is a healthy diet? There seem to be a bewildering number of conflicting answers against a background of tempting new products, all advertised as "natural", "healthy" and "wholesome". What are the real facts?

FOOD FASHIONS

With the development of nutritional science over the last 100 years, the major nutrients – protein, fat, carbohydrate, vitamins and minerals – appear to have fallen in and out of favour. Shortly after the war, everyone was urged to eat more protein, but today we are told that the Western world consumes too much of this expensive energy source. Recently there has been a well-publicized debate about fats: is margarine better for you than butter? Carbohydrate, once the enemy of the slimming industry is now back in favour, as a result of the pro-fibre campaign. Yet sugar, another carbohydrate, has been blamed for tooth decay, obesity and adult-onset diabetes. Each of these fashions spawn a new "diet", which in turn encourages unbalanced eating.

GETTING THE BALANCE RIGHT

All the major nutrients have distinctive and important roles to play in our diet, and it is now clear that a healthy diet means eating not only the right quantity, but also the right type of each one (see pp. 90–93).

The Western diet is very high in fat, sugar and salt, and low in fibre, fresh fruit and vegetables. The guidelines for a healthy diet, summed up by the reports prepared by the National Advisory Committee on Nutrition Education and the Committee on Medical Aspects of Food Policy are:

●Eat more unrefined carbohydrates which contain fibre (see pp. 90–92).

●Eat more fresh fruit and vegetables, which contain fibre as well as vitamins and minerals.

●Eat less fat, sugar and salt (see pp. 90–92).

Adopting a healthy diet that will positively help your long- and short-term health is, therefore, only a shift of emphasis, which can quickly become a way of life.

WHAT IS WRONG WITH A HIGH-FAT DIET?

High-fat diets have been clearly linked with incidence of coronary heart disease. Moreover, a high-fat diet tends to be a low-fibre diet, which is associated with intestinal disorders, constipation, diverticulitis and cancer of the colon. One further danger – on a high-fat diet, it is easy to consume excess calories, as fat contains more than twice the number of calories, weight for weight, as carbohydrate and protein. Surplus fat is stored in the body as fatty deposits, which can lead to obesity and its attendant problems of diabetes, high blood pressure and gall bladder disease. It is important to cut down your fat intake to about 30–35 per cent of the day's calories or less. There are three types of fat, which need to be distinguished according to their origin and their interaction with cholesterol.

SATURATED FATS
Mainly found in foods from animal sources (particularly red meat fat, full-fat cheeses, butter and cream), saturated fats are high in cholesterol and if they are eaten in excess, the cholesterol can be laid down as fatty deposits in the blood vessels which can lead to heart disease and atherosclerosis.

POLYUNSATURATED FATS
These fats are mainly found in foods from vegetable sources in liquid oil form usually from plant seeds, such as sunflower and safflower. They are, however, also present in solid form in grains and nuts. Although they contribute to the overall fat intake, they can lower levels of cholesterol in the blood.

MONOUNSATURATED FATS

These fats, which are found in olive oil, have no effect on cholesterol levels, but do add to daily fat intake.

The three types of fat are present in varying proportions in high-fat foods. The fat in butter, for example, contains 63 per cent saturated fat and only 3 per cent polyunsaturated, whereas the fat in polyunsaturated margarine contains 65 per cent polyunsaturated and 12 per cent saturated fat.

WHAT IS WRONG WITH A SUGAR-RICH DIET?

Sugar, or sucrose, in the form of refined white or brown sugar is all too easy to eat, but contributes only calories to a diet. Sugar not used immediately for fuel is converted into fat, encouraging weight gain. Sugar is also a principle factor in tooth decay. Highly refined carbohydrates, particularly sugar are also absorbed easily into the bloodstream, quickly increasing blood sugar levels. If the body overreacts to this, the blood sugar levels drop dramatically, leaving the desire to eat something sweet and thus creating a vicious circle. In addition, the cells that produce insulin cannot always cope with sudden concentrations of glucose and diabetes may result. Try not only to cut down on sugar in drinks and cooking, but when cutting down, take particular care to avoid manufactured foods, both sweet and savoury, where sugar comes near the top of the list of ingredients. Always check the nutritional labelling on the container.

WHY DO WE NEED LESS SALT?

There is a clear link in certain people between salt intakes and high blood pressure – a condition that can lead to circulatory problems, such as heart disease and strokes. The sodium from salt works with potassium in regulating body fluids. Excess salt upsets this balance, which puts a strain on the kidneys. In general, we eat more salt than we need. Do be aware of the amount hidden in processed foods and try not to add more during home cooking.

WHAT IS SO GOOD ABOUT FIBRE?

High-fibre foods are more filling than other foods, take longer to chew and satisfy hunger for longer, which reduces the temptation to eat between meals. They are also less completely digested, thus helping to reduce actual calorie intake. The evidence strongly suggests that lack of dietary fibre can cause cancer of the colon in addition to simple constipation. A low-fibre diet often means a high-fat, high-sugar diet with the problems that induces, including adult-onset diabetes. Only plant foods, in the form of unrefined carbohydrates, like whole grains and fresh fruit and vegetables, contain fibre and it is critical to eat more. Simply switching to high-fibre breakfast cereals, from refined flours and pastas to wholemeal, in addition to eating plenty of fresh fruit and vegetables will dramatically increase your fibre intake.

Sarah Brown

USING WHOLEFOODS

The first step in a healthy diet is to choose fresh and wholefoods that are unrefined and as close to their natural state as possible. Simply buy plenty of fresh fruit and vegetables, and use wholemeal flour, bread, pasta and pastry and health foods and whole grains, such as beans and oatmeal. When buying convenience food, select those that contain natural ingredients and the minimum of artificial colours, flavourings and preservatives. These steps alone will ensure that your diet is high in unrefined carbohydrate, rich in vitamins and minerals and lower in fat, salt and sugar.

USING THIS BOOK

The aim of this book is to translate the simple rules for health into a practical and enjoyable form. The recipes are naturally low in fat, high in fibre and unrefined ingredients, with natural sweeteners replacing sugar. Ingredients are used in their most nutritious form.

Healthy eating is not boring, nor does it involve a sacrifice. It is simply a matter of choosing and using more nutritious foods to create delicious, yet healthy meals.

USING THE RIGHT EQUIPMENT

● A blender will save a lot of time when mixing liquids, making fruit or vegetable purées or grinding nuts into a paste. It is ideal for making soups, smooth dips, fillings and frothy drinks.

● A food processor is more sophisticated. It comes with a variety of attachments for mincing, grating, shredding, dicing, mixing, juice extracting, puréeing and blending.

● If you do not have either, you will need a selection of sharp knives (including a serrated knife, a paring knife, a narrow salad knife and a cleaver), an electric grinder, a sieve, a palette knife, a whisk, a wooden spoon and a large mixing bowl.

USING HEALTHY ALTERNATIVES

● Use yogurt, smetana, silken tofu and low-fat soft cheeses instead of full-fat cheeses and cream.

● Use concentrated apple juice, honey, and dried fruit purées as an alternative sweetener to white or brown sugar.

HOW TO STORE FRUIT

● Keep the following in the fridge: apples, apricots, ripe avocados, cherries, peaches, pears, grapes, pineapple (if ripe and cut), raspberries, strawberries and melons.

● Store the following in a cool place (not the fridge): bananas, grapefruit, lemons, unripe pineapples, oranges, mandarins, passion fruit and mangoes.

● Eat tropical and soft fruits within 2–4 days of ripening.

● Keep citrus fruits for up to 3 weeks.

● Keep dried fruit for up to a year in an airtight container, but preferably use within 6 months (or before the "best before" date).

● When freezing fruit, use whole fruit within a year and pulped fruit within 6 months.

HOW TO STORE VEGETABLES

● Do not store vegetables in polythene.

● Always store in a cool, dark place as light and warmth destroy crispness and nutrients.

● Do not store the following, but eat as soon as possible after purchase: green vegetables, peas and beans, courgettes, aubergines, shoots, mushrooms and sweetcorn.

● Keep the following in cool conditions for up to 3 weeks: carrots, potatoes and onions.

● Store blanched vegetables in a freezer and use within a year.

HOW TO STORE NUTS AND SEEDS

● Store nuts in their shells where possible; they will keep for 6 months if stored in a cool place, or longer if frozen.

● Keep seeds and shelled nuts in an airtight container for not longer than 3 months. They will go rancid quite quickly if left in a warm place.

● Use ready-prepared (ground, chopped, flaked) nuts in 4–6 weeks.

USING FLAVOURINGS

● Use fresh herbs and whole spices where possible, but if you only have dried available, remember you only need half the quantity.

INGREDIENTS

Part of the joy of cooking is choosing the ingredients – especially when this involves selecting fresh fruit, herbs and vegetables and trying out new, unusual and exotic foods.

Always buy the freshest ingredients possible – they contain more vitamins and minerals and have a much better flavour and texture than preserved foods. Grains, pulses, flours, cereals and dried fruit, herbs and spices, however, generally keep for at least 3 months, so it is worth maintaining a small store of basic dry ingredients, particularly those that need to be soaked or cooked in advance. It is also useful to keep a small selection of canned or bottled fruit, vegetables and beans for emergencies. But try to select those without artificial additives or a high sugar or salt content and use them by the "best before" date.

The range of "healthy" ingredients has grown dramatically in recent years, particularly low-fat, reduced sugar, reduced salt, high fibre and vegetarian alternatives to traditional foods. These open the way to both a healthier and a more varied diet and offer endless possibilities for personal variations. The success of a recipe depends as much on the quality of the raw materials as on the way you combine them. In many cases, it is better to use a fresh alternative than to use the specified ingredient if it is not at its best – use fresh, ripe peaches, for example, in place of hard or over-ripe nectarines.

The following pages illustrate many of the familiar and the unusual ingredients found in the recipes in this book – from staples, to flavourings and dairy products. The section acts as both an identification guide and a reference source. You will find advice on choosing and storing food, together with useful information about the origins, culinary applications and nutritional value of specific ingredients. For more detailed nutritional information, see pages 90–93.

SALAD LEAVES

All salad leaves are low in calories and high in vitamins and minerals, especially Vitamins A and C and folic acid. Always buy firm, fresh-looking lettuces and wipe rather than wash them to retain the nutrients and flavour.

RED CABBAGE

A winter vegetable, red cabbage adds vivid colour, a crunchy texture and Vitamin C to a green salad.

LOVAGE

The entire lovage plant is edible and the leaves add a delicate, aromatic flavour to salads.

CHICORY

Obtainable through the winter, chicory is crisp and slightly bitter. Choose the whitest available.

SPINACH

Rich in iron and folic acid, spinach makes a sharp, nutritious salad leaf.

CHINESE LEAVES

This lightly crunchy salad of Chinese origin is found year-round. It should be handled gently and carefully wiped before eating.

RADICCHIO

This Italian red chicory is high in folic acid and adds colour and a slightly bitter flavour to salads.

WATERCRESS

More than just a garnish, watercress lends a peppery flavour to summer salads and boosts the calcium and folic acid content.

CURLY ENDIVE (frisé)

Known as chicory in America and chicoré in France, the slightly sharp-tasting, spiky leaves make an attractive salad base and add vitamins and minerals.

VINE LEAVES

Often stuffed and served as dolmades, vine leaves are also good shredded in salads.

OAKLEAF LETTUCE

Feuille de chêne is an appealing, jagged-leaved, heartless lettuce from France.

NASTURTIUM LEAVES

The leaves of this common garden plant make an unusual, delicately-flavoured addition to salads.

COS LETTUCE

Cos or romaine lettuce, which is slightly sharper and coarser than other varieties, is available year-round.

CABBAGE LETTUCE

The standard, round lettuce is always available, but with more plentiful supplies in the summer. It should have a large, firm heart and unblemished leaves.

GARDEN CRESS

Often sown with mustard, cress is a fast-sprouting, fresh-tasting ingredient, easily grown at home.

LAMB'S LETTUCE

These soft, velvety leaves, otherwise known as corn salad, make a delicious alternative to greenhouse lettuce in the winter.

PAK-CHOI

Also known as Chinese cabbage, pak-choi is like crisp, subtly-flavoured spinach and is available most of the year.

ICEBERG LETTUCE

The crispest and sweetest of lettuces, iceberg is also densely packed, so that the quantity of salad compensates for the higher price.

ROOTS, SHOOTS ᴬᴺᴰ SPROUTS

*Roots, shoots and sprouts are an inexpensive and nutritious element in
raw dishes. All are high in minerals, vitamins and fibre and beansprouts
contain valuable protein. Choose the freshest, firmest vegetables
available and store them in a cool, dark place, since light and heat can
reduce Vitamins B_2 and C, as well as crispness.*

ADUKI BEAN SPROUTS

Protein-rich, with a slight
peanut flavour, the
"Prince of beans" is
thought to have a
tonic effect.

COMMERCIALLY GROWN MUNG BEAN SPROUTS

The commercial variety are grown
in ideal conditions and should be
eaten the day they are bought.

CHICK PEA SPROUTS

Rich in protein and high in
magnesium, these sprouts make a
nutritious, nutty flavoured salad
ingredient.

HOME GROWN MUNG BEAN SPROUTS

Home grown sprouts reach their
peak nutritional value about $2\frac{1}{2}$
days after germination and can be
kept in the fridge for 3–4 days.

GARLIC

This pungent relation of
the onion family,
available year-round,
should be bought when
plump and fresh.

SPRING ONIONS

The immature bulb and shoot of
the common onion makes an
aromatic addition to salads. Welsh
onions, a separate variety, are
sometimes available.

BRUSSELS SPROUTS

These winter "miniature cabbages"
originated near Brussels in the Middle
Ages. They are rich in folic acid and
taste best when small and young.

MANGETOUT

These delicate vegetables, sometimes
called "sugar peas", are eaten whole.
Choose bright green, juicy pods.

CELERIAC

This much neglected, celery-flavoured tuber should be firm and solid. It needs to be peeled and, to avoid discolouration when cut, rubbed with lemon juice.

CELERY

Pascal celery has green ribs and dark green leaves; Golden celery has white ribs, yellow leaves, a crisper texture and better flavour. Both are available year-round.

MOOLI

Also known as daikon and winter radish, this mild white Japanese radish has more nutritional value than red spring ones.

FENNEL

Available year-round, fennel has a crisp, aniseed-flavoured bulb and herb-like leaves. Store in the fridge.

KOHLRABI

This German "cabbage turnip" comes with a red or green root and is rich in Vitamin C. It should be eaten when young, crisp and tender.

RADISHES

Early spring radishes have a less peppery flavour than later crops. Store in iced water in the fridge for a crisp texture.

WHITE TURNIPS

Turnips vary in size, shape and colour. Although found at all times of year, the young, early summer, round roots from France are the sweetest.

SEEDS, NUTS AND CEREALS

Nuts and cereals are important staples in a healthy diet, providing protein, fibre, unsaturated fats and essential vitamins and minerals. Unshelled nuts (available in the winter months) keep indefinitely, but shelled nuts (always available) should be stored in a cool, dry place or a freezer. Unsalted nuts last longer than salted. Wheatgerm must be kept refrigerated and used within two months.

SESAME SEEDS

These oily seeds from the Indian plant, *Sesamum indicum*, are used to make tahini.

ROLLED OAT FLAKES

(rolled oats, porridge oats)

Oat flakes are made from whole oat grains, pressed and broken by rolling.

WHEATGERM

The protein- and vitamin-rich embryo of the wheat grain should be used within 2 months before it turns rancid. Stabilized wheatgerm keeps longer.

SUNFLOWER SEEDS

The seeds from the sunflower plant are rich in unsaturated oils, protein and minerals.

OLIVES

There are 35 species of olive tree, yielding a variety of fruit. Green olives are simply unripe black ones.

RYE FLAKES

Stronger in colour and flavour than oat or wheat flakes, rye is high in B Vitamins, potassium and magnesium.

PINHEAD OATMEAL

Dehusked oats are ground to produce fine, medium (pinhead) or coarse oatmeal, which makes a nutritious topping for desserts.

PUMPKIN SEEDS

The flat green seeds of the pumpkin are delicious roasted and are rich in protein, oil and minerals, especially zinc.

PINE KERNELS

The seeds of the Mediterranean stone pine tree are roasted and make a good snack or topping for salads.

ALMONDS

Sweet almonds contain more protein than any other nut and can be served whole, crushed or ground into a paste. Bitter almonds are distilled into almond essence.

CASHEWS

Although usually sold shelled and salted, healthier, unsalted cashews are available.

PISTACHIO

Bright green pistachio nuts are usually sold in their shells. To preserve the natural colour, shell, boil and skin the nuts.

WALNUTS

Ripe brown walnuts are a rich source of protein and unsaturated fat. Green, unripe Vitamin C-rich walnuts are usually pickled.

HAZELNUTS

Also known as cobs or filberts, hazelnuts contain less fat than any other nut. Put shelled nuts under the grill for a few minutes before peeling.

PECAN NUTS

A relative of the walnut, this nut is rich in vitamins and minerals. Stand in boiling water for 15–20 minutes before shelling.

FRUIT

Fresh fruit is an excellent source of Vitamin C, natural sugar (fructose), fibre and many minerals. More exotic fruits are becoming widely available and some fresh fruits can now be bought year-round. For the best flavours and prices, however, it is wise to buy fresh fruit in season and opt for canned, frozen or dried varieties at other times of year.

RASPBERRIES

There are two raspberry crops, one in summer and one in autumn, but frozen raspberries are available year-round.

ORANGES

Blood oranges have thinner skins and redder flesh, while navel oranges have thicker skins than normal oranges (above left).

APRICOTS

Fresh apricots are in season through late spring and summer. The stronger the colour, the sweeter the flavour.

PLUMS

Dessert plums are sweeter and juicier than cooking plums, although both can be eaten raw. Choose plums without bruises and with perfect skins.

PEACHES

There are many varieties of peach, including nectarines – smooth-skinned peaches.

GRAPEFRUIT

Pink grapefruit are much sweeter than the more usual white variety (above). When crossed with a tangerine, it becomes an ugli.

PINEAPPLE

When ripe, fresh pineapples have a sweet smell and easily detached leaves. Eat within a few days of ripening. Choose canned pineapple in natural juice as an alternative.

APPLES

Of the many varieties of dessert apple, Cox's Orange Pippin (above) has perhaps the best flavour and Red Delicious the best colour for raw dishes.

MANGO

The large red-skinned mango and the two green-skinned types are all rich in Vitamin A.

HONEYDEW MELON

Winter melons, such as Honeydew, have smooth skins; Canteloupe and Ogens have a "netted" skin.

WATERMELON

Made up of 91 per cent water, watermelons are low in calories. They keep for a week in the fridge.

DRIED BANANAS

Bananas are dried whole or in long slices (right); or sliced and fried to make banana chips.

DRIED DATES

Dried dessert dates are sold unpitted. Dried dates for cooking are sold in blocks.

SULTANAS

Sultanas, or dried white seedless grapes, are sweeter than raisins. Where possible, choose those without a shiny surface.

DRIED FIGS

They can be eaten dry, or soaked in water and eaten reconstituted.

RAISINS

There are three types of raisin: seedless (left); juicier dessert Lexia raisins; and seeded Muscatel raisins with a stronger flavour.

FRESH DATES

The best are plump and moist with thin skins. They freeze well and so are available year-round.

YELLOW PEPPER

Sweet yellow peppers are a variety of the green capsicums that turn red when ripe. All are high in Vitamin C and are not to be confused with hot chilli peppers.

AVOCADO

Only available fresh, the smooth, green-skinned avocado (above) and the rough, black-skinned variety both have oily, Vitamin C-rich flesh.

PEARS

The many types of pear available include the dessert pears, Packham (above), William, Comice and Conference. Eat as soon as possible after ripening.

HERBS, SPICES AND FLAVOURINGS

Herbs, spices and flavourings add vitamins and minerals, as well as natural flavour to uncooked food. To conserve the full taste, use fresh herbs and whole spices, but if only dried herbs and ground spices are available, store them in an airtight container. Oregano, marjoram, sage, bay leaf and dill are much better dried than parsley, chives, chervil and fennel leaves.

CINNAMON
(sticks)
Available in sticks or as powder, cinnamon is the dried bark of an Indian tree.

TAHINI
A thick, oily paste made from sesame seeds, that is rich in calcium and high in protein.

SHOYU
(natural soya sauce)
Shoyu is a high-protein, sugar-free flavouring.

MISO PASTE
Miso, a protein-rich paste, is made from the slow, natural fermentation of soya beans and barley.

GINGER
Root ginger can be bought whole, sliced or ground.

CUMIN
Available whole or ground, cumin seeds have a distinctly hot, bitter flavour.

CARDAMOM PODS
The green pods from a ginger-related plant contain dark, spicy seeds.

PAPRIKA
The ground seeds of the sweet red or green pepper, *capsicum annuum*, are mildly spicy.

CHILLI PEPPERS
Dried, ripe chilli peppers are very hot and keep well.

GREEN PEPPERCORNS
Berries of the pepper tree, *piper nigrum*, are often pickled when still green.

CELERY SEEDS
The seeds of the celery plant add a slightly bitter flavour to salads and cold soups.

WHOLEGRAIN MUSTARD
Whole mustard seeds are mixed with wine, pepper and allspice.

HORSERADISH
This grated root is a pungent flavouring.

CAPERS
These small buds are pickled in vinegar.

DILL WEED
The leaves of dill, an annual plant, are available fresh in the summer months and dried at other times.

TARRAGON
The leaves of this perennial southern European plant are available fresh, dried or ground. French tarragon has a more distinct flavour than other varieties.

CHIVES
Related to the onion family, chive stems are finely chopped in soups and salads.

CORIANDER
The fresh leaves have a fresh, fruity flavour and are available dried.

BASIL
There are several varieties, including sweet and bush basil, but all have a clove-like flavour when fresh and a hotter flavour when dried.

CONCENTRATED APPLE JUICE
This Vitamin C-rich fruit juice concentrate makes an excellent natural sweetener in place of sugar.

PARSLEY
Both curled (above) and flat parsley are rich in iron and Vitamin C. Dried parsley is available, but has less flavour than fresh.

BAY LEAVES
The aromatic leaves of the sweet bay tree are more often available dried than fresh.

DAIRY PRODUCE
AND ALTERNATIVES

*Low-fat cheeses and milks and their soya-based alternatives mean that
"dairy products" can contribute protein, calcium and Vitamins A and
D to a healthy diet without adding extra saturated fat. Keep cheeses and
milk in the fridge, sealed from the air, and eat soft and curd cheeses and
yogurt soon after purchase.*

COTTAGE CHEESE

This low-fat, granular cheese is made
from the separated curds of skimmed
milk and is excellent with salads and
fruit. A half-fat variety is also available.

RICOTTA CHEESE

Made from the whey of separated
cow's (or sheep's) milk, ricotta is
low in fat but has a soft, creamy texture.

SMETANA

(5–10 per cent fat)
A low-fat substitute for cream,
smetana is made from a mixture
of skimmed milk and single
cream.

CHEDDAR

Cheddars come in a variety of colours, and
maturity. There are low-fat and vegetarian
(rennet-free) varieties.

SOFT TOFU

Made from the curds of the soya bean,
tofu comes soft-pressed (above), firm
(below) or smooth (silken tofu).

CURD CHEESE

(11 per cent fat)
This medium-fat soft cheese
is made from the
separated curds of whole
milk.

YOGURT

Made from whole or skimmed milk
and left to ferment under
controlled conditions by the action
of bacteria. Greek strained yogurt is
more concentrated.

FIRM TOFU

Protein-rich and low in fat, tofu makes
a nutritious main ingredient and
quickly absorbs other flavours.

SKIMMED MILK SOFT CHEESE

(quark)
Quark is made from semi-skimmed milk and contains
no salt. It is sharper and smoother than curd cheese.

STARTERS

Raw starters are quick and easy to prepare.
A refreshing cold soup or a spicy dip, for
example, whets the appetite and can be
chosen to complement the protein, fibre,
vitamins and minerals in the main course.

TOFU AND TOMATO SOUP

INGREDIENTS
1 red pepper, deseeded
4 tomatoes
4 spring onions
1 × 10oz (300g) packet silken tofu
2 tbsp (30ml) tomato purée
dash of Tabasco
1/4 pint (150ml) tomato juice
(or as required)
salt and pepper

GARNISH
sesame seeds

•
NUTRITION PROFILE
*This soup is low in calories and is a good
source of Vitamin C, calcium and copper.*

• Per portion •
Carbohydrate: 7.2g
Protein: 7.2g **Fibre:** 3.2g
Fat: 6.2g **Calories:** 110

*Tofu's creamy texture is useful for soups and blends well with soft fruit
and vegetables. For a good colour, choose red tomatoes and add extra
purée and, for a smooth texture, skin the pepper. If you prefer a thinner
mixture, add a little more tomato juice.*

Preparation time: 20 mins (plus chilling time)
Serves 4

METHOD

1. Roast the pepper under a low grill until the skin has charred
and will peel off.

2. Scald the tomatoes in boiling water and carefully peel off the
loosened skin with a sharp knife. Then chop into small pieces.
Trim and chop the spring onions.

3. In a food processor or blender, blend the skinned pepper with
all the remaining ingredients until smooth.

4. Season to taste and sprinkle some sesame seeds on top.
Serve chilled.

Illustrated on page 22

AVOCADO ~ LETTUCE SOUP

INGREDIENTS

½ pint (300ml) natural yogurt
1 ripe avocado, peeled and stoned
juice of 1 lemon
½ pint (300ml) water
salt and pepper
4oz (125g) crisp lettuce
2 tbsp (30ml) chopped chives

•

NUTRITION PROFILE

*This soup is rich in Vitamins B₂, C and E,
folic acid, calcium and polyunsaturated
fats.*

• Per portion •
Carbohydrate: 6.6g
Protein: 6.3g   **Fibre:** 2.9g
Fat: 12g   **Calories:** 155

*Avocado gives a wonderful flavour and rich creamy texture to cold
summer soups, especially when combined with yogurt. The avocado
can be watered down considerably to reduce the fat content, without
impairing the flavour.*

Preparation time: 20 mins (plus chilling time)
Serves 4

METHOD

1. In a blender, mix together the yogurt, avocado and lemon juice
to a smooth paste.

2. Add the water gradually until the mixture has a pouring
consistency. Season to taste.

3. Cut the lettuce into fine shreds and mix it into the soup, then
add the chives.

4. Serve chilled.

Illustrated opposite

CUCUMBER ~ ORANGE SOUP

INGREDIENTS

⅔ cucumber
salt
4 oranges
juice of 1–2 lemons
½ pint (300ml) peppermint tea, cold

GARNISH
sprig of mint

•

NUTRITION PROFILE

*This soup is low in calories, contains
virtually no fat, and is high in Vitamin C.*

• Per portion •
Carbohydrate: 10.3g
Protein: 2.1g   **Fibre:** 3.6g
Fat: 0.1g   **Calories:** 50

*A very refreshing, low-fat starter for summer days, this soup is thirst-
quenching and easy to digest. The slices of orange and cucumber add to
the texture of the soup.*

Preparation time: 30 mins (plus chilling time)
Serves 4

METHOD

1. Peel the cucumber and slice into slivers. Lay on a flat plate,
sprinkle with salt, weigh down with another plate and leave for
20 minutes.

2. Peel 2 oranges and cut into very thin slices.

3. Squeeze the juice from the remaining 2 oranges and mix it with
the lemon juice and peppermint tea.

4. Rinse the cucumber. Mix it into the fruited mint mixture, then
add the orange slices. Garnish with mint. Serve chilled.

Illustrated opposite

Clockwise from top: **Avocado and lettuce soup** (*see above*);
Tofu and tomato soup (*see p. 21*); **Cucumber and orange soup** (*see above*).

RASPBERRY AND ALMOND SOUP

INGREDIENTS
2 egg yolks
1 tbsp (15ml) pear and apple spread
1 pint (600ml) skimmed milk
4oz (125g) skimmed milk soft cheese
(quark)
3 drops almond essence
8oz (250g) raspberries

GARNISH
toasted almonds

•

NUTRITION PROFILE
This soup is high in protein and fibre, contains Vitamins B$_2$, B$_{12}$ and D, and is also a good source of Vitamins C and E, calcium, magnesium and zinc.

• Per Portion •
Carbohydrate: 14g
Protein: 11.7g **Fibre:** 4.6g
Fat: 3.3g **Calories:** 135

This creamy soup makes an unusual starter or dessert. It is sweet and rich-tasting, yet contains no sugar and, if you use low-fat milk and low-fat soft cheese, is not too high in fat. The sweetness comes from pear and apple spread. As an alternative, use honey.

Preparation time: 30 mins (plus chilling time)
Serves 4

METHOD

1. Whisk together the egg yolks and pear and apple spread for about 5 minutes or until light and frothy.

2. Add the milk very gradually, whisking continuously. Then beat in the cheese and the almond essence to taste.

3. Rinse the raspberries and divide between 4 soup cups, then pour in the almond cream.

4. Serve chilled, garnished with toasted almonds.

Illustrated opposite

GAZPACHO

INGREDIENTS
½ small cucumber, peeled and cubed
6 tomatoes, skinned and diced
6 spring onions, trimmed and chopped
1 clove garlic, crushed
1 tbsp (15ml) red wine vinegar
1 tbsp (15ml) olive oil
2 tbsp (30ml) finely chopped fresh
parsley
¾ pint (450ml) tomato juice
¼ tsp ground cinnamon
6 cloves
1 bay leaf
½ tsp shoyu

•

NUTRITION PROFILE
This soup is high in fibre, low in fat and calories, and rich in Vitamins A and C.

• Per portion •
Carbohydrate: 9.2g
Protein: 2.6g **Fibre:** 4.3g
Fat: 3.8g **Calories:** 80

This soup tastes rich, yet is healthily low in fat and high in fibre. For a good strong flavour, use tomato juice as a base. To be sure the other flavours develop, leave the soup for a couple of hours before serving.

Preparation time: 20 mins (plus 2 hours standing time)
Serves 4

METHOD

1. Prepare the vegetables and mix together in a large bowl.

2. Add the remaining ingredients and mix together gently but thoroughly.

3. Allow the soup to stand for 2 hours, then remove the bay leaf and cloves before serving.

Illustrated opposite

Top: **Raspberry and almond soup** (*see above*);
Bottom: **Gazpacho** (*see above*).

AVOCADO AND CORIANDER DIP

INGREDIENTS

1 avocado, peeled and stoned
juice of ½ lemon
5 tbsp (75ml) natural yogurt
2 tbsp (30ml) finely chopped fresh
coriander leaves
salt and pepper

GARNISH
slice of lemon
slice of lime

•

NUTRITION PROFILE

*This dip is rich in Vitamin E, calcium and
polyunsaturated fats.*

• Per portion •
Carbohydrate: 2.5g
Protein: 4.2g **Fibre:** 1.7g
Fat: 11.6g **Calories:** 135

*The smooth texture of avocado and its delicate colour make it an ideal
base for dips. It is rich, however, so use it sparingly.*

Preparation time: 15 mins (plus 1 hour standing time)
Serves 3–4

METHOD

1. In a blender, mix the avocado with the lemon juice and yogurt
until completely smooth.

2. Stir in the coriander.

3. Season to taste, then leave the dip to stand for about an hour
to allow the flavours to develop.

4. Garnish with a slice of lemon and a slice of lime and serve with
crudités (strips of raw vegetables).

Illustrated opposite

SAVOURY CASHEW CREAM

INGREDIENTS

4oz (125g) cashew nuts
up to ⅓ pint (200ml) water
2 tsp (10ml) finely chopped fresh
marjoram
1–2 tsp (5–10ml) shoyu

•

NUTRITION PROFILE

*This cream is a good source of magnesium
and protein.*

• Per portion •
Carbohydrate: 5.8g
Protein: 5g **Fibre:** 1.5g
Fat: 13.3g **Calories:** 166

*Nut dressings and creams are ideal as dips, salad dressings or as sauces
for stuffed vegetables or rissoles. They are all made by adding liquid to a
ground nut base and will thicken when left to stand.*

Preparation time: 10 mins
Serves 6

METHOD

1. In a blender or food processor, grind the cashew nuts
thoroughly to a fine powder.

2. Add the water gradually, stirring continuously, to form
a thick cream.

3. Add marjoram and shoyu to flavour.

4. Leave to stand for 1–2 hours before serving.

Illustrated opposite

Clockwise from top: **Cucumber dip with dill** (*see p.28*); **Avocado and coriander dip** (*see above*); **Hot Spanish dip** (*see p.28*);
Savoury cashew cream (*see above*).

HOT SPANISH DIP

INGREDIENTS

2 tomatoes, skinned
½ green pepper, deseeded
½ red pepper, deseeded
1 green chilli pepper, deseeded
2 tbsp (30ml) olive oil
1 tbsp (15ml) red wine
1–2 cloves garlic, crushed

GARNISH
sprig of mint

•

NUTRITION PROFILE

This dip is a good source of Vitamin C.

• Per portion •
Carbohydrate: 2.4g
Protein: 0.8g **Fibre:** 0.7g
Fat: 7.7g **Calories:** 85

The vivid colour and strong taste make this dip a welcome low-calorie addition to any salad table. The vegetables need to be chopped very finely, to produce a smooth texture.

Preparation time: 20 mins
Serves 4

METHOD

1. Prepare all the vegetables and chop very finely or mince.

2. In a bowl, mix the olive oil, red wine and garlic, add to the vegetables and stir thoroughly.

3. Season to taste. Garnish with mint and serve with courgette crudités and black olives.

Illustrated on page 27

CUCUMBER DIP WITH DILL

INGREDIENTS

4oz (125g) skimmed milk soft cheese
(quark)
6 tbsp (90ml) natural yogurt
¼ cucumber, peeled and finely diced
1 tsp (5ml) dried dill weed
1 tbsp (15ml) lemon juice
salt and pepper

GARNISH
sprig of dill

•

NUTRITION PROFILE

Very low in calories and fat, this dip is also a good source of protein and calcium.

• Per portion •
Carbohydrate: 3.1g
Protein: 5.4g **Fibre:** 0.2g
Fat: 0.3g **Calories:** 35

The combination of quark and yogurt makes a low-fat yet creamy base for a dip and contributes a surprising amount of protein. The texture of the cucumber complements the refreshing watermelon and green-bean crudités.

Preparation time: 10 mins (plus chilling time)
Serves 4

METHOD

1. In a blender, mix together the quark and yogurt.

2. Add the finely diced cucumber, the dill weed and lemon juice.

3. Season to taste, garnish with dill and serve chilled with chunks of watermelon and green beans.

Illustrated on page 27

SPROUTED CHICK PEA DIP

INGREDIENTS

6oz (175g) chick pea sprouts (see below)
2 tbsp (30ml) tahini
2 tbsp (30ml) lemon juice
2 tsp (10ml) shoyu
¼ tsp cumin seeds
2 cloves garlic, crushed

•

NUTRITION PROFILE

A good source of Vitamins B_1 and C, iron, magnesium and zinc, but not high in calories. Crudités increase Vitamin C.

• Per portion •
Carbohydrate: 4.5g
Protein: 3.9g **Fibre:** 3.1g
Fat: 4.1g **Calories:** 65

The delicious fresh flavour of chick pea sprouts increases when they are ground, and blends well with the accompanying flavours. You will get the freshest taste if you grow your own (see below). For an alternative version, try adding more herbs and reducing the shoyu.

Preparation time: 15 mins
Serves 4

METHOD

1. Rinse the sprouts and grind them thoroughly in a blender or food processor.

2. Add the remaining ingredients and grind again until fairly smooth.

3. Serve with cucumber, peppers and tomatoes.

Illustrated on page 30

SPROUTING BEANS

Sprouting your own beans is cheap and easy, and by using them when they are young and fresh, you can have the full benefit of their high vitamin and mineral content. The following are particularly easy to grow: mung beans, aduki beans, alfalfa, mustard and cress, whole lentils. Where possible, buy organically grown seeds. One handful of seeds will yield about eight handfuls of sprouts. Salad sprouters, which allow you to grow three varieties of seed, are available.

1. Put 2 tbsp (30ml) seeds in a large jam jar and fill it with water. Soak the seeds overnight, then drain away the water.

2. Cover the jar with a piece of muslin, secured with an elastic band and keep in a warm place. Every morning and evening pour lukewarm water through the muslin to rinse the beans, then drain them well.

3. After each rinse, leave the jar upside down to ensure that all the water has drained away. After 2–3 days, put the jar in sunlight for a day or two until the beans are sprouted and continue to rinse with water.

CRUNCHY ORANGE DIP

INGREDIENTS

4oz (125g) skimmed milk soft cheese
(quark)
6 tbsp (90ml) natural yogurt
rind and juice of 1 orange
1oz (25g) sesame seeds
1 tsp (5ml) coriander seeds
½ tsp rock salt
black pepper

•

NUTRITION PROFILE

*This dip is high in protein and contains
Vitamin C and calcium.*

• Per portion •
Carbohydrate: 4.5g
Protein: 7.3g **Fibre:** 1.6g
Fat: 3.8g **Calories:** 80

*Sharp citrus flavours go well with a smooth quark base and make a good
acid/alkali balance. Here, roasted sesame and coriander seeds add
flavour, texture and protein to the dip.*

Preparation time: 15 mins
Serves 4

METHOD

1. In a blender, mix together the quark, yogurt, orange
rind and juice.

2. Roast the sesame and coriander seeds in a heavy pan for 2–3
minutes to bring out the flavour.

3. Grind with the salt using a pestle and mortar.

4. Mix the roasted seeds and salt into the quark dip.

5. Season with black pepper and serve with chicory and
satsuma segments.

Illustrated opposite

TOFU DIP

INGREDIENTS

½ × 10oz (300g) packet silken tofu
1 tbsp (15ml) olive oil
1 tsp (5ml) shoyu
1 clove garlic, crushed
½ tsp sesame oil
salt and pepper

•

NUTRITION PROFILE

*A good source of polyunsaturated fats, this
dip is also high in calcium and copper.*

• Per portion •
Carbohydrate: 1.7g
Protein: 1.9g **Fibre:** – –
Fat: 0.1g **Calories:** 60

*Creamy in texture, low in fat, high in protein, and receptive to other
flavours, tofu (bean curd) is ideal as a dip or dressing. Silken tofu, the
smoothest type, made from a mixture of curds and whey, is the most
suitable for dips.*

Preparation time: 10 mins
Serves 4

METHOD

1. In a blender, mix the silken tofu with the olive oil and shoyu.

2. Add the garlic to the tofu with the sesame oil. Blend again
until smooth.

3. Season to taste.

Illustrated opposite

Clockwise from top left: **Sprouted chick pea dip** (*see p.29*); **Tofu dip** (*see above*); **Crunchy orange dip** (*see above*).

MUSHROOM AND WALNUT DIP

INGREDIENTS

4oz (125g) mushrooms, wiped and
chopped
2oz (50g) walnuts
3 spring onions, trimmed and chopped
1 tbsp (15ml) sunflower oil
1 clove garlic, crushed
1 tsp (5ml) paprika
4 tsp (20ml) shoyu
1 tsp (5ml) dried marjoram
4 tsp (20ml) red wine vinegar
2 tsp (10ml) tahini
4–5 tbsp (60–75ml) water

•

NUTRITION PROFILE

*This dip is rich in Vitamin E and
polyunsaturated fats.*

• Per portion •
Carbohydrate: 2.4g
Protein: 2.9g **Fibre:** 2.3g
Fat: 12g **Calories:** 130

*Mushrooms are delicious raw and add colour to dips, while walnuts
contribute texture, flavour and protein. This recipe could be served
with carrot and turnip crudités or be used as a savoury spread.*

Preparation time: 20 mins
Serves 4

METHOD

1. Grind the mushrooms and walnuts together in a blender or
food processor.

2. Add the spring onions, oil, garlic, paprika, shoyu, marjoram
and vinegar and blend.

3. In a bowl, mix the tahini and water together until smooth.

4. Blend the diluted tahini thoroughly with the rest of the dip.
Serve with crudités.

Illustrated opposite

COTTAGE CHEESE AND PINEAPPLE DIP

INGREDIENTS

3oz (75g) cottage cheese
2 tbsp (30ml) natural yogurt
1 tbsp (15ml) mayonnaise
2 tsp (10ml) sunflower oil
2 tbsp (30ml) pineapple juice

•

NUTRITION PROFILE

*This dip contains Vitamin E and calcium
and is not as high in calories and fat as you
may think.*

• Per portion •
Carbohydrate: 1.4g
Protein: 3g **Fibre:** 0.1g
Fat: 6.3g **Calories:** 75

*It is a good idea to reduce the fat content of this rich, creamy dip by
using low-fat cottage cheese and low-calorie mayonnaise. To ensure a
smooth, grainless result, blend all the ingredients thoroughly.*

Preparation time: 15 mins
Serves: 4

METHOD

1. In a blender, mix the cottage cheese with the yogurt
until very smooth.

2. Add the remaining ingredients and blend until smooth.

3. Serve with chunks of pineapple, radicchio and mangetout.

Illustrated opposite

Clockwise from top right: **Mushroom and walnut dip** (*see above*); **Fresh tomato relish** (*see p. 34*);
Tahini and apricot relish (*see p. 34*); **Cottage cheese and pineapple dip** (*see above*).

TAHINI AND APRICOT RELISH

INGREDIENTS

2oz (50g) dried apricots, soaked
1 onion, peeled and chopped
1 small green pepper, deseeded and
chopped
½ chilli pepper, deseeded and diced
2 tbsp (30ml) cider vinegar
1 tsp (5ml) tahini
•

NUTRITION PROFILE

*This low-calorie relish is high in fibre,
Vitamin C and potassium, yet free from
added sugar and salt.*

• Per portion •
Carbohydrate: 7.5g
Protein: 1.8g **Fibre:** 4.3g
Fat: 1.6g **Calories:** 50

*Quick to prepare and free from refined sugar, additives and
preservatives, this relish makes a tasty accompaniment to savoury
rissoles and loaves or use it as a chunky salad dressing.*

Preparation time: 10 mins (plus overnight soaking time)
Serves 4

METHOD

1. Drain the apricots and slice finely.

2. Prepare the onion, pepper and chilli and mix with the apricots.

3. Add the vinegar, then mix in the tahini.

4. Serve immediately.

Illustrated on page 33

FRESH TOMATO RELISH

INGREDIENTS

3oz (75g) dried stoned dates
4oz (125g) dried apple rings
1 small onion, peeled and finely
chopped
2–3 tbsp (30–45ml) red wine vinegar
3 tomatoes, skinned and chopped
2 tbsp (30ml) tomato purée
½ inch (1cm) fresh root ginger, peeled
and grated
½ tsp allspice
½ tsp mustard seeds
black pepper
•

NUTRITION PROFILE

*High in fibre and low in fat, this relish is
also rich in Vitamin C.*

• Per portion •
Carbohydrate: 34.2g
Protein: 2.2g **Fibre:** 6g
Fat: 0.3g **Calories:** 145

*Home-made relishes lend spice and moisture to nut and seed snacks and
to chunky vegetable salads. They are easy to prepare and can be sugar-,
salt- and additive-free.*

Preparation time: 30 mins
Serves 4

METHOD

1. Finely chop or mince the dates and apple rings.

2. Mix with the onion.

3. In a blender or food processor, mix the vinegar, tomatoes and
tomato purée together until smooth.

4. Mix the tomato sauce with the fruit mixture and add the spices
and seasoning to taste.

5. Keep in the fridge and use within 5–6 days.

Illustrated on page 33

MAIN COURSES

These main course dishes are infinitely versatile. A light, leafy salad can become a substantial meal when served with a generous dressing and plenty of fresh bread, while a rich nut loaf, stuffed vegetables or a chunky, protein-rich salad can be scaled down to make a nutritious starter.

STUFFED CUCUMBER
WITH CHICK PEA SPROUTS AND COTTAGE CHEESE

INGREDIENTS

2oz (50g) chick pea sprouts (see p.29)
4oz (125g) cottage cheese
1 tbsp (15ml) lemon juice
$\frac{1}{2}$ tsp fresh basil
$\frac{1}{4}$ tsp fennel seeds
$\frac{1}{2}$ tsp fresh rosemary
$\frac{1}{4}$ tsp turmeric
salt and pepper
1 large cucumber

GARNISH
watercress

•

NUTRITION PROFILE

This low-fat, low-calorie dish is a good source of Vitamin C.

• Per portion •
Carbohydrate: 4.3g
Protein: 5.6g **Fibre:** 1g
Fat: 1.5g **Calories:** 55

Chick pea sprouts – which are high in fibre, vitamins and minerals – give substance to this low-calorie filling. Other sprouts, such as lentils, would make a good alternative. If you prefer to use dried herbs, halve the quantities.

Preparation time: 30 mins
Serves 4

METHOD

1. In a blender or food processor, grind the chick pea sprouts with the cottage cheese, lemon juice, herbs and spices. Season to taste.

2. Slice the cucumber in half along its length and scoop out the seeds from the centre.

3. Fill the hollow with the cheese mixture and slice into 2 inch (5cm) chunks.

4. Serve with a few sprigs of watercress.

Illustrated on page 37

STUFFED ICEBERG LETTUCE
WITH PECANS ~ CHEESE

INGREDIENTS

1 iceberg lettuce
4oz (125g) ricotta
2 tbsp (30ml) natural yogurt
1oz (25g) pecan nuts
1oz (25g) sultanas
2oz (50g) fresh redcurrants
salt and pepper

•

NUTRITION PROFILE

This recipe provides a good supply of Vitamins A, B$_{12}$ and C; also calcium, iron and folic acid.

• Per portion •
Carbohydrate: 8.6g
Protein: 8.3g **Fibre:** 4.7g
Fat: 11.3g **Calories:** 165

An unusual way of serving lettuce, this makes a surprisingly nutritious meal. If you want to keep the calories low, use a low-fat ricotta or a curd cheese. If fresh redcurrants are not available, use frozen.

Preparation time: 20 mins
Serves 4

METHOD

1. Slice a lid off the top of the iceberg lettuce and cut out the centre, leaving a generous shell (see below). Put the inner part of the lettuce aside.

2. Mix together the ricotta and yogurt in a bowl. Add the pecan nuts, sultanas, and half the redcurrants. Season to taste.

3. Spoon the cheese mixture into the lettuce shell and pack down with a spoon.

4. Garnish with the remaining redcurrants. Shred the inner part of the lettuce and use it as a bed for the filled shell. Refrigerate and when serving use a sharp knife to cut into portions.

Illustrated opposite

MAKING A LETTUCE SHELL

Vegetables can make beautiful decorative cases for a dish. You can either scoop out the centre, mix it with other ingredients as a filling, and then spoon it back into the shell, for example using peppers, tomatoes or courgettes; or you can use the centre as a decoration around the outside of the shell, for example using iceberg lettuce. Both methods enable you to benefit from all the goodness of the vegetable in an economical and attractive way. To ensure the casing is firm, chill the vegetable before filling it.

1. Slice a lid off the top of the iceberg lettuce, using a sharp knife.

2. Cut down inside the lettuce and scoop out the centre, leaving a thick shell to contain a filling.

3. Shred the scooped-out centre of the lettuce and use it as a bed for the stuffed lettuce.

Top: **Stuffed cucumber with chick pea sprouts and cottage cheese** (*see p.35*);
Bottom: **Stuffed iceberg lettuce with pecans and cheese** (*see above*).

PEPPERS STUFFED WITH ALMONDS

INGREDIENTS

2 large green or red peppers

SAUCE

2 tomatoes, skinned and chopped
2oz (50g) ground almonds
1 tsp (5ml) red wine vinegar
1 tsp (5ml) tomato purée
pinch chilli powder

FILLING

2oz (50g) fresh black olives, stoned and chopped
1 tomato, chopped
2 sticks celery, diced

•

NUTRITION PROFILE

This recipe is rich in Vitamins C and E.

• Per portion •
Carbohydrate: 3.5g
Protein: 3.4g   **Fibre:** 3.8g
Fat: 8.4g   **Calories:** 100

Nut creams taste rich but are not high in cholesterol and make a healthy alternative to mayonnaise. The crunchy sweetness of the raw peppers complements the smooth savoury sauce.

Preparation time: 30 mins
Serves 4

METHOD

1. Wash the peppers, slice in half across the width and deseed.

2. For the sauce, mix all the sauce ingredients in a blender or food processor until completely smooth. Season to taste.

3. For the filling, prepare the olives, tomato and celery, and stir into the almond sauce.

4. Divide the filling into four and spoon into each pepper half. Garnish with coriander and serve immediately.

Illustrated on page 40

STUFFED TOMATOES
WITH BULGAR WHEAT, FENNEL AND PINE KERNELS

INGREDIENTS

4 large tomatoes
2oz (50g) bulgar wheat
4 fl oz (125ml) water
6oz (175g) fennel
2oz (50g) pine kernels
1oz (25g) currants
2 tbsp (30ml) red wine vinegar
1 tbsp (15ml) olive oil
4 tbsp (60ml) chopped fresh parsley
1 tsp (5ml) shoyu
salt and pepper

•

NUTRITION PROFILE

High in Vitamins A and C, this dish also provides plenty of dietary fibre.

• Per portion •
Carbohydrate: 17g
Protein: 4.7g   **Fibre:** 4.9g
Fat: 11.6g   **Calories:** 175g

The strong flavour and texture of bulgar wheat makes it a useful high-fibre addition to salads and vegetable stuffings.

Preparation time: 35 mins
Serves 4

METHOD

1. Slice a lid off each tomato and scoop out the inner flesh and seeds.

2. Put the bulgar wheat in a medium-sized bowl, boil the water and pour over the wheat. Allow to stand for 15–20 minutes.

3. Meanwhile trim and dice the fennel.

4. Mix the fennel, pine kernels, currants, vinegar, oil, parsley and shoyu into the bulgar wheat and season to taste.

5. Fill each tomato with the mixture, garnish with a sprig of mint and serve at room temperature.

Illustrated on page 40

STUFFED VINE LEAVES
WITH OLIVE PASTE

INGREDIENTS

4oz (125g) fresh black olives
1 tbsp (15ml) lemon juice
2 spring onions, trimmed and chopped
2 tomatoes, skinned and chopped
1 tsp (5ml) dried oregano
¼ tsp celery seeds
1 clove garlic, crushed
1–2 tsp (5–10ml) brandy
1oz (25g) rye flakes
1–2 tbsp (15–30ml) tahini
12–14 vine leaves

•

NUTRITION PROFILE

This dish is a good source of iron, magnesium and Vitamin C; it is also rich in calcium, copper and Vitamin A.

• Per portion •
Carbohydrate: 7.6g
Protein: 4.4g **Fibre:** 3.4g
Fat: 6.4g **Calories:** 110

A variation on a classic Greek dish, these savoury mouthfuls make a good high-fibre, low-fat meal. The strong flavour of the olive paste combines well with vine leaves and the tahini helps to offset the acidity of the other ingredients.

Preparation time: 40 mins (plus 1 hour standing time)
Serves 4

METHOD

1. Stone the olives and chop into small pieces.

2. In a blender, mix all the ingredients except the rye flakes, tahini and vine leaves. Season to taste.

3. Stir in the rye flakes and leave to stand for 1 hour.

4. Stir in the tahini. This will thicken the mixture slightly.

5. Rinse the vine leaves. Put a heaped dessertspoon of olive paste in the centre of each leaf and roll up (see below). Serve with a wedge of lemon.

Illustrated on page 40

STUFFING VINE LEAVES

Stuffed vine leaves, known as Dolmades in Greece and Dolmas in Turkey, are a traditional Middle-Eastern dish, in which a savoury filling is wrapped in a parcel of vine leaves and served hot or cold. The leaves are available in Britain, fresh or canned and preserved in brine. You could use blanched cabbage and spinach leaves in the same way.

1. Remove the stalk and put a dessertspoon of filling into the centre of each leaf.

2. Start folding the base and left side of the leaf over the filling.

3. Fold the right side of the leaf over the filling and roll the leaf away from you to form a neat package.

HAZELNUT AND PAPRIKA LOAF

INGREDIENTS

4oz (125g) hazelnuts
4oz (125g) carrots, scrubbed and grated
4oz (125g) onions, peeled and chopped
4oz (125g) porridge oats
1 tsp (5ml) chopped fresh sage
1 tsp (5ml) chopped fresh thyme
1 tsp (5ml) French mustard
1 tsp (5ml) sunflower oil
2 fl oz (50ml) water or yeast
extract stock

GARNISH
paprika

•

NUTRITION PROFILE

*High in fibre, this loaf is also a rich source
of Vitamins A and E, zinc, magnesium,
iron and folic acid.*

• Per portion •
Carbohydrate: 26.9g
Protein: 6.5g **Fibre:** 5g
Fat: 15.2g **Calories:** 265

*This nut loaf makes a nutritious and satisfying meal. Of all the nuts,
hazelnuts are the lowest in fat and still contain a good balance of
protein, vitamins and minerals. For a pleasant moist texture and to
limit the calories, add a good quantity of water – the nuts will retain
their flavour and the mixture will firm up on standing.*

Preparation time: 30 mins (plus 1 hour standing time)
Serves 4

METHOD

1. In a nut mill or food processor, grind the hazelnuts finely.

2. Add the grated carrot, chopped onion, oats, herbs, mustard
and oil. Blend until the ingredients are thoroughly mixed.

3. Gradually add the water or stock and blend until the mixture is
just wet enough to hold together. It will firm up when left.

4. Season to taste. Pack into a loaf tin, lined with greaseproof
paper. Leave to stand for one hour, then turn out and dust with
paprika. Serve with cress and cherry tomatoes.

Illustrated on page 42

MIXED SEED RISSOLES

INGREDIENTS

2oz (50g) pumpkin seeds
2oz (50g) sunflower seeds
2oz (50g) sesame seeds
2 sticks celery, trimmed and diced
1/4 tsp cumin seeds
1/4 tsp turmeric
4 tsp (20ml) lemon juice
1 tsp (5ml) shoyu

GARNISH
3–4 tbsp (45–60ml) finely chopped
fresh parsley

•

NUTRITION PROFILE

*These rissoles are a good source of
Vitamins C and E, magnesium and zinc.*

• Per portion •
Carbohydrate: 4.9g
Protein: 10.1g **Fibre:** 2.6g
Fat: 18.8g **Calories:** 220

*Pumpkin, sesame and sunflower seeds make an excellent nutritional
mix—high in protein, vitamins and minerals. The spices add extra
flavour to the crunchy consistency of the seeds and celery.*

Preparation time: 20 mins
Makes 4 × 2oz (50g) rissoles

METHOD

1. Grind the seeds thoroughly in a food processor or nut mill.

2. Add the celery, spices, lemon juice, shoyu and season to taste.

3. Mix in a food processor or blender until the mixture begins to
bind together.

4. Shape into rissoles and coat in fresh parsley.

5. Serve with salad, dill and slices of cucumber.

Illustrated on page 42

Clockwise from top left: **Stuffed vine leaves with olive paste** (*see p.39*); **Stuffed tomatoes with bulgar wheat, fennel
and pine kernels** (*see p.38*); **Peppers stuffed with almonds** (*see p.38*).

CHEESE AND HERB BALLS

INGREDIENTS

8oz (250g) curd cheese
2 tbsp (30ml) wheatgerm
1 clove garlic, crushed
4 spring onions, trimmed and finely chopped
1 tbsp (15ml) chopped fresh parsley
1 tbsp (15ml) chopped fresh chives
1 tbsp (15ml) chopped fresh tarragon
salt and pepper

COATING
1oz (25g) unsalted peanuts, ground
1 tbsp (15ml) wheatgerm

•

NUTRITION PROFILE

These high-fibre balls are rich in Vitamins C, B_{12} and E.

• Per portion •
Carbohydrate: 7.2g
Protein: 6.8g   **Fibre:** 5.2g
Fat: 6.1g   **Calories:** 110

The firm texture of curd cheese is ideal as a base for savoury or sweet balls. Fresh herbs and wheatgerm add extra nutrients as well as flavour. Alternatively, you could create your own variations by adding spices, seeds or dried fruits. This dish looks attractive served on a bed of endive and garnished with sliced cherry tomatoes.

Preparation time: 15 mins
Serves 4

METHOD

1. In a food processor or blender, mix the curd cheese with the wheatgerm and garlic.

2. Add the finely chopped spring onions and herbs, mix well. Season to taste.

3. Shape into small balls and coat in a mixture of ground peanuts and wheatgerm.

Illustrated opposite

WALDORF SALAD

INGREDIENTS

4 sticks celery, trimmed
4oz (125g) fresh dates, stoned
2 red apples
2oz (50g) Cheddar cheese
6 tbsp (90ml) mayonnaise
6 tbsp (90ml) natural yogurt
1 tsp (5ml) caraway seeds
12 walnut halves

GARNISH
celery leaf

•

NUTRITION PROFILE

This salad is a rich source of calcium and contains Vitamins D and E.

• Per portion •
Carbohydrate: 15.2g
Protein: 6.1g   **Fibre:** 2.1g
Fat: 26.6g   **Calories:** 325

The caraway not only lifts the flavour, but helps the digestion of the rich dressing. If you use Cheddar, slice it thinly so that it goes a long way. If you want to reduce the fat and calorie content, use a low-calorie mayonnaise and low-fat cheese.

Preparation time: 20 mins
Serves 4

METHOD

1. Cut the celery on the diagonal into coarse pieces.

2. Roughly chop the dates and apples.

3. Cut the cheese into very thin slices.

4. Mix together the mayonnaise, yogurt, caraway seeds and walnut halves. Combine all the ingredients. Season to taste and garnish with the celery leaf.

Illustrated on page 45

Clockwise from top left: **Mixed seed rissoles** (*see p.41*); **Hazelnut and paprika loaf** (*see p.41*);
Cheese and herb balls (*see above*).

SPIKY BEETROOT SALAD
WITH AVOCADO DRESSING

INGREDIENTS

4 large sticks celery, trimmed
8oz (250g) raw beetroot, peeled
8oz (250g) carrots, peeled
juice of ½ lemon
1 tsp (5ml) concentrated apple juice or honey

DRESSING

1 avocado, peeled and stoned
juice of 1 large lemon
2 tbsp (30ml) natural yogurt
2 cloves garlic, crushed
1 tsp (5ml) concentrated apple juice or honey
salt and pepper
•

NUTRITION PROFILE

This is a high-fibre salad, rich in Vitamins A, B_6, C and E, folic acid and copper.

• Per portion •
Carbohydrate: 11.5g
Protein: 4.1g **Fibre:** 9.1g
Fat: 11.2g **Calories:** 160

It is worth trying raw beetroot – it has a distinctive flavour and is more nutritious than cooked. The sharp, yet creamy avocado dressing balances and complements the crunchy texture of the three vegetables.

Preparation time: 25 mins
Serves 4

METHOD

1. Cut the celery, beetroot and carrot into julienne strips.

2. Combine the lemon juice and concentrated apple juice.

3. Toss the beetroot and carrots separately in the mixture to keep them fresh.

4. For the dressing, blend the avocado with the remaining ingredients and garnish with a coriander leaf.

5. Arrange clusters of celery, beetroot and carrot strips clockwise around a large circular plate. Then garnish the centre of the plate with lamb's and oakleaf lettuce leaves.

Illustrated opposite

FRUIT SALAD COCKTAIL
WITH CURRIED MAYONNAISE

INGREDIENTS

½ pineapple
1 lb (500g) watermelon, peeled
2oz (50g) mung bean sprouts
¼ cucumber

DRESSING

4 tbsp (60ml) curried mayonnaise (see p. 70)
•

NUTRITION PROFILE

This is a good source of Vitamins C and E.

• Per portion •
Carbohydrate: 18.7g
Protein: 2.2g **Fibre:** 2.5g
Fat: 14.7g **Calories:** 210

Clean but spicy, a savoury fruit salad makes a refreshing low-calorie accompaniment to a bean or nut dip (see pp. 26, 29, 32). Try sprouting your own mung beans from seed (see p. 29).

Preparation time: 20 mins
Serves 4

METHOD

1. Peel the fruit and cut into coarse chunks.

2. Rinse the bean sprouts.

3. Cut the cucumber into chunks.

4. Mix all the ingredients together in a large bowl and stir in the dressing.

Illustrated opposite

Clockwise from top: **Waldorf salad** (*see p.43*); **Avocado dressing** (*see above*); **Spiky beetroot salad** (*see above*); **Fruit salad cocktail with curried mayonnaise** (*see above*).

AUTUMN MEDLEY

INGREDIENTS

6oz (175g) broccoli, trimmed
6oz (175g) fennel, trimmed
4oz (125g) turnip, scrubbed or peeled
6oz (175g) carrots, scrubbed or peeled
6oz (175g) Brussels sprouts, trimmed

DRESSING
4–5 tbsp (60–75ml) apple juice
2 tbsp (30ml) tahini
$\frac{1}{2}$ tsp shoyu
1 tsp (5ml) lemon juice
salt and pepper

•

NUTRITION PROFILE

High in iron, folic acid, calcium, magnesium, zinc and fibre, this salad is also rich in Vitamins A and C.

• Per portion •
Carbohydrate: 8.9g
Protein: 6.6g   **Fibre:** 7.2g
Fat: 4.9g   **Calories:** 100

Winter vegetables, although not normally associated with salads, can be just as good raw as summer produce, and equally nutritious. Remember, however, to cut those with stronger flavours into small pieces as large chunks can be overpowering.

Preparation time: 25 mins
Serves 4

METHOD

1. Cut the broccoli into small spears, the fennel into thin strips, the turnips and carrots into round slices and the sprouts into quarters and mix together in a large bowl.

2. For the dressing, mix the apple juice gradually into the tahini, then add the remaining ingredients and season to taste.

3. Pour the dressing over the salad and mix thoroughly.

Illustrated opposite

GREEK SALAD

INGREDIENTS

7oz (200g) feta cheese, cubed
$\frac{1}{2}$ cucumber, diced
20 fresh black olives, stoned and chopped
4 small tomatoes, halved
1 green pepper, deseeded and sliced into strips
juice of 1 lemon

GARNISH
sprig of mint

•

NUTRITION PROFILE

This salad contains Vitamin B_{12} and is also a good source of Vitamins A, C and E, calcium and folic acid.

• Per portion •
Carbohydrate: 4.7g
Protein: 10.6g   **Fibre:** 3.5g
Fat: 12.2g   **Calories:** 160

The feta cheese makes this a substantial main course and its strong flavour is well complemented by the olives and the plain lemon juice dressing. Try serving with warm wholemeal pitta bread, for a balanced main course.

Preparation time: 15 mins
Serves 4

METHOD

1. Prepare all the salad ingredients and mix together in a large bowl.

2. Toss in lemon juice and garnish with fresh mint.

Illustrated opposite

From top: **Spanish salad with tomato dressing** (*see p.49*); **Greek salad** (*see above*); **Autumn medley** (*see above*).

SPANISH SALAD WITH TOMATO DRESSING

INGREDIENTS

1 small onion, peeled
1 green pepper, deseeded
4oz (125g) courgettes, wiped
1 small avocado, peeled
4 medium tomatoes

DRESSING
2 tomatoes, skinned and chopped
1 tbsp (15ml) tomato purée
juice of ½ lemon
1 tbsp (15ml) olive oil
½ tsp chopped fresh oregano
½ tsp chopped fresh thyme
2 cloves garlic, chopped

GARNISH
sprig of oregano
•

NUTRITION PROFILE

*This salad is a good source of Vitamins A,
B_6, C and E and of iron and folic acid.*

• Per portion •
Carbohydrate: 7.1g
Protein: 3.9g **Fibre:** 3.2g
Fat: 11g **Calories:** 140

*The light tomato dressing enhances the flavour of the vegetables and if
you have any left over, try using it as a base for Gazpacho.*

Preparation time: 25 mins
Serves 4

METHOD

1. Slice the onion into very thin rings.

2. Cut the pepper into rings.

3. Cut the courgettes, avocado and tomatoes into fine slices.

4. For the dressing, blend the tomatoes, purée and lemon juice.
Then add the oil and herbs.

5. Mix in the garlic. Season to taste.

6. Toss all the salad ingredients together and pour the dressing
over the top. Garnish with a sprig of oregano or marjoram.

Illustrated on page 47

TABBOULEH

INGREDIENTS

6oz (175g) bulgar wheat
pinch salt
½ pint (300ml) boiling water
½ cucumber, diced
4 tbsp (60ml) finely chopped fresh mint
4 tbsp (60ml) finely chopped fresh
parsley

DRESSING
2 tbsp (30ml) olive oil
2 tbsp (30ml) lemon juice
•

NUTRITION PROFILE

*This high-fibre dish is also a good source of
Vitamin C.*
Carbohydrate: 34.5g
Protein: 5.8g **Fibre:** 5.2g
Fat: 8.2g **Calories:** 230

*This delicious, satisfying dish is very simple to prepare. The nutty-
tasting bulgar wheat provides a strong base for the predominating
flavour of fresh herbs. To keep the calorie and fat content low, this
recipe has less oil than the traditional version.*

Preparation time: 15 mins (plus 30 mins cooling time)
Serves 4

METHOD

1. Mix the bulgar wheat with the salt.

2. Pour on the boiling water and leave it to cool.

3. Once cold, mix in the cucumber, mint and parsley.

4. Mix together the olive oil and lemon juice and toss into
the salad.

Illustrated opposite

Top: **Tabbouleh** (*see above*); Bottom: **Mushroom salad with minty horseradish sauce** (*see p.50*).

MUSHROOM SALAD
WITH MINTY HORSERADISH SAUCE

INGREDIENTS

12oz (375g) baby button mushrooms
2 tbsp (30ml) creamed horseradish
3–4 tbsp (45–60ml) natural yogurt
1 tbsp (15ml) finely chopped fresh mint
salt and pepper

GARNISH
sprig of mint
•

NUTRITION PROFILE

This low-fat salad is also a good source of copper and niacin.

• Per portion •
Carbohydrate: 1.8g
Protein: 2.6g Fibre: 2.4g
Fat: 2.1g Calories: 40

A simple, low-calorie salad with a delicious subtle flavour and smooth texture. Wipe rather than wash the mushrooms, or you will lose valuable vitamins.

Preparation time: 15 mins
Serves 4

METHOD

1. Carefully wipe the mushrooms with a damp cloth. Cut them in quarters or if they are very small, leave them whole.

2. Mix together the horseradish, yogurt and mint and season to taste. Mix into the mushrooms. Garnish with mint and serve.

Illustrated on page 48

TRADITIONAL COLESLAW
WITH YOGURT ᴬᴺᴰ MUSTARD DRESSING

INGREDIENTS

8oz (250g) white cabbage, shredded
4oz (125g) carrots, scrubbed and grated
2oz (50g) unsalted peanuts
3 spring onions, trimmed and coarsely chopped

DRESSING
6 tbsp (90ml) mayonnaise
6 tbsp (90ml) natural yogurt
1 tsp (5ml) wholegrain mustard
salt and pepper

GARNISH
watercress
•

NUTRITION PROFILE

This high-protein salad is a rich source of Vitamins A, C and E. It also contains folic acid and some Vitamin B_{12}.

• Per portion •
Carbohydrate: 7g
Protein: 6.4g Fibre: 3.9g
Fat: 27.4g Calories: 300

The sweetness of carrots complements the crispness of cabbage and makes a good colour contrast. Peanuts add protein and texture and the onions and mustard sharpen the flavour. If you want to reduce the calorie content, use a low-calorie mayonnaise.

Preparation time: 25 mins
Serves 4

METHOD

1. Prepare the cabbage and carrots. Mix well with the nuts and spring onions.

2. Mix the dressing ingredients together and toss into the salad.

3. Serve at room temperature on a bed of crisp lettuce, garnished with watercress.

Illustrated opposite

From top: **Winter slaw** (*see* p.53); **Lentil coleslaw** (*see* p.52);
Traditional coleslaw with yogurt and mustard dressing (*see* above).

BEETROOT SLAW
WITH ORANGE AND SESAME DRESSING

INGREDIENTS
2oz (50g) raisins
juice of ½ orange
8–10oz (250–300g) raw baby
beetroot, peeled
2 tbsp (30ml) finely chopped chives

DRESSING
juice of 1½ oranges
1 tsp (5ml) orange rind
1 tbsp (15ml) sunflower oil
1 tsp (5ml) sesame oil
1 clove garlic, crushed
½ tsp celery seeds

•

NUTRITION PROFILE

*This slaw contains plenty of Vitamins
C and E.*

• Per portion •
Carbohydrate: 22.2g
Protein: 1.7g   **Fibre:** 3.4g
Fat: 5g   **Calories:** 135

*Baby beetroots are sweet and delicious raw and have a flavour that
blends well with the dried fruits. If you have time, soak the raisins in
fruit juice for the best end results.*

Preparation time: 20 mins (plus 1–2 hours soaking time)
Serves 4

METHOD

1. Soak the raisins in orange juice for 1–2 hours.

2. Prepare the beetroot and grate finely.

3. Mix in the raisins and chives.

4. For the dressing, mix the ingredients together and toss into the
salad.

Illustrated on page 55

LENTIL COLESLAW

INGREDIENTS
8oz (250g) white cabbage, shredded
4oz (125g) lentil sprouts (see p.29)
2 spring onions, trimmed and chopped
2 tbsp (30ml) finely chopped fresh
parsley
3 tbsp (45ml) French dressing (see
p.72)

•

NUTRITION PROFILE

*This salad contains a good quantity of
Vitamins C and E.*

• Per portion •
Carbohydrate: 4.1g
Protein: 2.8g   **Fibre:** 3.2g
Fat: 2g   **Calories:** 45

*High in protein and fibre, this nutritious coleslaw is best eaten
immediately after making while it is still fresh and crisp.*

Preparation time: 20 mins
Serves 4

METHOD

1. Prepare the cabbage.

2. Mix with the lentil sprouts, onions and parsley.

3. Toss well in the dressing.

Illustrated on page 51

WINTER SLAW

INGREDIENTS

8oz (250g) carrots, peeled or scrubbed
4oz (125g) turnip, peeled
4oz (125g) swede, peeled
2 tbsp (30ml) tahini
6 tbsp (90ml) water
1 tsp (5ml) wholegrain mustard
½ tsp creamed horseradish
salt and pepper

GARNISH
sprig of coriander

•

NUTRITION PROFILE

Relatively low in fat and calories, this salad is rich in Vitamins A and C.

• Per portion •
Carbohydrate: 6.5g
Protein: 3.4g **Fibre:** 3.5g
Fat: 4.9g **Calories:** 80

Root vegetables are high in fibre and full of valuable vitamins and minerals. They are often associated with casseroles and stews, but are delicious raw and when mixed together create an interesting combination of colour and flavour.

Preparation time: 20 mins
Serves 4

METHOD

1. Grate the raw vegetables into fine strands and mix together.

2. In a separate bowl, mix the tahini with 2 tbsp (30ml) of the water, beating well until smooth. Add the remaining water gradually.

3. Add the mustard and horseradish to the tahini. Season to taste.

4. Mix the dressing into the salad and serve immediately.

Illustrated on page 51

RED CABBAGE SLAW
WITH A SWEET ∾ SOUR DRESSING

INGREDIENTS

10oz (300g) red cabbage, finely shredded
4oz (125g) dried dates, stoned and chopped
1oz (25g) pumpkin seeds

DRESSING
1 tbsp (15ml) sunflower oil
1 tbsp (15ml) lemon juice
1 tbsp (15ml) red wine vinegar
1 tbsp (15ml) concentrated apple juice
2 tsp (10ml) capers, finely chopped
1 tsp (5ml) wholegrain mustard
1 tsp (5ml) clear honey

•

NUTRITION PROFILE

This salad contains folic acid and is rich in Vitamins E and C.

• Per portion •
Carbohydrate: 26g
Protein: 3.4g **Fibre:** 3.6g
Fat: 6.6g **Calories:** 170

The strong flavour of red cabbage goes well with fruit, especially dates or raisins, and is enhanced by a sweet sauce and the nutty taste of pumpkin seeds. Red cabbage is tougher than white and needs to be cut into very fine shreds.

Preparation time: 20 mins
Serves 4

METHOD

1. Prepare the cabbage and dates. Mix with the pumpkin seeds in a large bowl.

2. For the dressing, combine all the ingredients together. Season to taste.

3. Mix the dressing into the slaw and serve immediately.

Illustrated on page 55

CREAMED CELERIAC SALAD

INGREDIENTS

8–10oz (250–300g) celeriac
1 red apple
2oz (50g) chopped mixed nuts
3–4 tbsp (45–60ml) smetana
juice of ½ lemon
pinch turmeric
salt and pepper

•

NUTRITION PROFILE

This salad contains small but useful amounts of iron, calcium and Vitamins E and C.

• Per portion •
Carbohydrate: 6.3g
Protein: 4.7g   **Fibre:** 4.6g
Fat: 7.2g   **Calories:** 105

Celeriac may look ugly on the outside, but its skin masks a deliciously crunchy vegetable with a celery flavour. You will need to toss it in dressing soon after peeling to prevent the white flesh discolouring.

Preparation time: 20 mins
Serves 4

METHOD

1. Peel the celeriac and grate finely.

2. Slice and core the apple, then cut it into thin slivers and mix with the celeriac and nuts.

3. Mix the smetana, lemon juice and turmeric together, season to taste and add to the celeriac. Garnish with slices of apple.

Illustrated opposite

CLASSIC GREEN SALAD

INGREDIENTS

1 small lettuce heart
1 small crisp lettuce
¼ cucumber, sliced
4 spring onions, trimmed
1 small bunch watercress
4–5 sprigs fresh lovage

DRESSING
1 tbsp (15ml) olive oil
1–2 tbsp (15–30ml) lemon juice
large pinch mustard powder
¼ tsp celery seeds
1 tsp (5ml) concentrated apple juice
or clear honey
1 clove garlic, crushed
black pepper

•

NUTRITION PROFILE

Rich in iron, calcium, folic acid and Vitamins A and C, this simple salad is also low in fat and calories.

• Per portion •
Carbohydrate: 3.6g
Protein: 2.9g   **Fibre:** 4g
Fat: 4.4g   **Calories:** 65

Simple and inexpensive, a classic green salad with a variety of salad leaves and a good dressing makes a refreshing accompaniment to any dish. For variety, you could use endive, oakleaf lettuce or lamb's lettuce. Wiping salad leaves helps to keep them crisp and does not remove any nutrients.

Preparation time: 30 mins
Serves 4

METHOD

1. Select the best salad leaves, prepare them carefully, place in a large bowl and refrigerate.

2. Prepare the other salad ingredients and add to the salad leaves in the fridge.

3. Just before serving, toss the salad in the olive oil.

4. For the dressing, mix the remaining ingredients together and toss into the salad.

5. Serve immediately.

Illustrated on page 56

Clockwise from top: **Red cabbage slaw with a sweet and sour dressing** (*see p.53*); **Creamed celeriac salad** (*see above*); **Beetroot slaw with orange and sesame dressing** (*see p.52*).

ALFALFA SALAD
WITH MARINATED MUSHROOMS

INGREDIENTS
8oz (250g) cos lettuce leaves
4 tomatoes
2oz (50g) alfalfa sprouts (see p.29)

DRESSING
2 tbsp (30ml) white wine vinegar
4 tbsp (60ml) sunflower oil
2 spring onions, trimmed and finely
chopped
1 clove garlic, crushed
1oz (25g) mushrooms, wiped and finely
sliced
salt and pepper
•

NUTRITION PROFILE
This salad is rich in Vitamins A, C and E.

• Per portion •
Carbohydrate: 4g
Protein: 1.8g **Fibre:** 2.4g
Fat: 15.3g **Calories:** 160

Alfalfa sprouts add flavour, texture and extra vitamins and minerals to green salads. Try growing your own from seed (see p.29); it costs very little and is easy to do.

Preparation time: 15 mins (plus 2 hours marinating time)
Serves 4

METHOD

1. Wipe the lettuce leaves, cut the tomatoes into thin wedges and mix carefully with the alfalfa sprouts. Then refrigerate.

2. For the dressing, mix all the ingredients together and leave for 2 hours to marinate. Season to taste.

3. Just before serving the salad, toss in the dressing and serve immediately.

Illustrated opposite

CHICORY ᴬᴺᴰ GRAPEFRUIT SALAD

INGREDIENTS
1 pink grapefruit
8oz (250g) chicory, chopped
1 avocado, peeled and cubed
4oz (125g) mung bean sprouts

DRESSING
$\frac{1}{2}$ × 10oz (300g) packet silken tofu
2 tbsp (30ml) grapefruit juice
$\frac{1}{2}$ tsp shoyu
1 tsp (5ml) sesame oil
•

NUTRITION PROFILE
Rich in iron, copper, magnesium and folic acid, this salad also contains Vitamins C and E.

• Per portion •
Carbohydrate: 9.2g
Protein: 6.1g **Fibre:** 2.5g
Fat: 13.3g **Calories:** 180

The sweet taste of pink grapefruit and the smoothness of the avocado soften the sharpness of the chicory. The low-fat tofu dressing with a hint of sesame oil enhances the salad and enriches the texture and taste. Use ordinary grapefruit if pink is unavailable, but add a little orange juice to the dressing for sweetness.

Preparation time: 30 mins
Serves 4

METHOD

1. Halve the grapefruit. Cut the flesh of one half into small pieces and reserve the other half for the juice in the dressing.

2. Prepare the other salad ingredients and mix together.

3. For the dressing, mix all the ingredients in a blender or food processor until smooth.

4. Serve the salad with the dressing poured over the top.

Illustrated opposite

From top: **Alfalfa salad with marinated mushrooms** (*see above*); **Chicory and grapefruit salad** (*see above*);
Classic green salad (*see p.54*).

GREEN SALAD WITH RAVIGOTE DRESSING

INGREDIENTS

2oz (50g) dried apricots
1 punnet salad cress
2oz (50g) spinach
8oz (250g) crisp lettuce or endive

DRESSING

2 tbsp (30ml) chopped fresh parsley
3 spring onions, trimmed and chopped
½oz (15g) watercress, finely chopped
1 tbsp (15ml) capers
4 tsp (20ml) olive oil
4 tsp (20ml) white wine vinegar

•

NUTRITION PROFILE

This low-fat, low-calorie dish is high in dietary fibre and a good source of folic acid, calcium, iron and Vitamins A and C.

• Per portion •
Carbohydrate: 15.1g
Protein: 3.3g **Fibre:** 10.4g
Fat: 0.3g **Calories:** 75

This is a simplified adaptation of the classic French "ravigote" sauce. The ingredients contribute good quantities of essential vitamins and minerals. A little dried fruit adds sweetness and contrast to any leafy salad and, if you like the taste, consider using curly endive (frisé) instead of lettuce for variety.

Preparation time: 20 mins (plus soaking overnight)
Serves 4

METHOD

1. Soak the dried apricots overnight. Drain and cut into slivers.

2. Cut and wash the salad cress.

3. Shred the spinach and lettuce (or endive) into thin strips.

4. Mix all the salad together in a large bowl.

5. For the dressing, mix all the ingredients and toss into the salad just before serving.

Illustrated opposite

PAK-CHOI SALAD
WITH SHERRY AND SPICE DRESSING

INGREDIENTS

2oz (50g) sultanas
juice of ½ lemon
10oz (300g) pak-choi (leaf and stem)
4–6 large radishes
2oz (50g) mung bean sprouts (see p.29)

DRESSING

1 tbsp (15ml) lemon juice
1 tbsp (15ml) sunflower oil
1 tsp (5ml) shoyu
2 tsp (10ml) sherry
1 clove garlic, crushed
¼ tsp Chinese five-spice powder

•

NUTRITION PROFILE

This salad is rich in Vitamins A, C and E.

• Per portion •
Carbohydrate: 12.9g
Protein: 3.7g **Fibre:** 3.4g
Fat: 3.9g **Calories:** 100

Pak-choi is an oriental vegetable now becoming popular and more widely available in the West. The top leaves of this useful plant can be used raw in salads or stir-fried, and the stem makes a good, crunchy salad ingredient.

Preparation time: 45 mins (plus 1–2 hours soaking time)
Serves 4

METHOD

1. Soak the sultanas in the lemon juice for 1–2 hours.

2. Shred the stem of the pak-choi and a little leaf for contrast.

3. Slice the radishes thinly and rinse the mung bean sprouts.

4. Mix the sultanas and all the salad together in a large bowl.

5. For the dressing, mix all the ingredients together and toss into the salad. Serve immediately.

Illustrated opposite

Clockwise from top: **Green salad with ravigote dressing** (*see above*); **Mixed leaf salad** (*see p.61*); **Wheatberry salad with ginger dressing** (*see p.60*); **Pak-choi salad with sherry and spice dressing** (*see above*).

WHEATBERRY SALAD
WITH GINGER DRESSING

INGREDIENTS

4oz (125g) wheatberry sprouts (see p.29)
8oz (250g) Chinese leaves
1lb (500g) carrots, scrubbed
2 tbsp (30ml) sesame seeds
1 inch (2.5cm) fresh root ginger
¼ pint (150ml) natural yogurt
salt and pepper

•

NUTRITION PROFILE

A high-protein salad, this is also a good source of calcium, magnesium, folic acid and Vitamins A and C.

• Per portion •
Carbohydrate: 14g
Protein: 7.8g   **Fibre:** 4.7g
Fat: 4.6g   **Calories:** 125

The combination of distinct flavours and the good balance of nutrients makes this a useful main course salad. Try growing your own wheat grain or wheatberry sprouts and eat them small when they are sweetest.

Preparation time: 15 mins
Serves 4

METHOD

1. Rinse the wheatberry sprouts.

2. Shred the Chinese leaves, dice the carrots and mix with the sprouts and sesame seeds.

3. Peel the root ginger, chop it finely, and add to the yogurt.

4. Mix the yogurt and ginger into the salad and season to taste.

Illustrated on page 59

MAKING YOGURT

You can make yogurt from any kind of milk, even soya milk. Use commercial, live yogurt for the first batch and after that simply remember to reserve 2 tbsp (30ml) for successive batches. Yogurt is an extremely versatile ingredient: you can use it in soups, dips, dressings, as a healthy alternative to cream, and to make cottage cheese go further. It is an excellent source of protein and calcium and keeps for about one week in the fridge.

1. Put 1 pint (600ml) of skimmed milk in a pan and heat to 115°F (44°C).

2. Stir in 2 tbsp (30ml) of natural low-fat yogurt, pour the mixture into a warmed wide-rimmed thermos flask and leave overnight.

3. The following day, pour the yogurt out of the thermos into a bowl and store in the fridge, where it will set.

MIXED LEAF SALAD

INGREDIENTS

8oz (250g) lamb's lettuce
4oz (125g) oakleaf lettuce (feuille de chêne)
4oz (125g) sorrel leaves or spinach
1 small radicchio – about 4oz (125g)

DRESSING
1 tbsp (15ml) olive oil
2 tbsp (30ml) white wine vinegar
3 cloves garlic, finely chopped
$1/2$ tsp green peppercorns, crushed
1 bay leaf
2 tsp (10ml) fresh tarragon

•

NUTRITION PROFILE

This low calorie salad is a good source of Vitamins A and C, and contains folic acid.

• Per portion •
Carbohydrate: 4.3g
Protein: 3.1g **Fibre:** 3.5g
Fat: 4.2g **Calories:** 70

The exotic range of colours, textures and flavours now available in salad leaves have added fresh interest to simple salads. Oakleaf, sorrel and radicchio contribute colour, shape and a robust flavour, which offsets the softer, milder lamb's lettuce.

Preparation time: 25 mins
Serves 4

METHOD

1. Wipe the lamb's and oakleaf lettuces carefully.

2. Shred the sorrel and radicchio into fine strips.

3. Mix all the salad leaves in a large bowl, cover and refrigerate.

4. For the dressing, mix the ingredients together well.

5. Remove the bay leaf. Toss the dressing over the salad just before serving.

Illustrated on page 59

CALIFORNIAN SALAD
WITH TARRAGON DRESSING

INGREDIENTS

2 large peaches
6 radishes
1oz (25g) hazelnuts
4oz (125g) green beans, trimmed
$1/2$ punnet salad cress

DRESSING
1 tbsp (15ml) olive oil
1 tbsp (15ml) white wine vinegar
1 tsp (5ml) concentrated apple juice
1 tsp (5ml) shoyu
2 tsp (10ml) fresh tarragon

•

NUTRITION PROFILE

This salad is rich in Vitamins C and E and also contains Vitamin B_6 and zinc.

• Per portion •
Carbohydrate: 6.8g
Protein: 1.5g **Fibre:** 2.7g
Fat: 6g **Calories:** 85

Crunchy nuts, soft fruits and crisp vegetables create a wonderful combination of textures, flavours and nutrients. If you do not have the suggested combinations of root and shoot vegetables and fruits, try improvising with alternatives.

Preparation time: 20 mins
Serves 4

METHOD

1. Cut the peaches and radishes into thin slices.

2. Lightly toast the hazelnuts under a preheated grill for 2–3 minutes to bring out the flavour. Then slice.

3. Chop the beans into 1 inch (2.5cm) lengths. Cut the cress.

4. Mix all the salad ingredients together in a large bowl.

5. For the dressing, thoroughly mix the ingredients and pour over the salad.

Illustrated on page 62

FRUIT ~ FENNEL SALAD

INGREDIENTS

8oz (250g) seedless green grapes
12oz (375g) fennel, trimmed and
chopped
2oz (50g) blanched almonds, halved
4oz (125g) radicchio

DRESSING

¼ pint (150ml) natural yogurt
1–2 tsp (5–10ml) grated horseradish
¼ tsp turmeric or saffron infused in a
little water

•

NUTRITION PROFILE

*High in fibre, this salad is also rich in
Vitamins C and E.*

• Per portion •
Carbohydrate: 16.1g
Protein: 6.1g **Fibre:** 5.5g
Fat: 7.1g **Calories:** 155

*The dry, crisp taste of almonds combines well with the clean, aniseed
taste of fennel and the sweetness of the grapes. The low-calorie dressing
has a similar blend of piquant and refreshing flavours.*

Preparation time: 25 mins
Serves 4

METHOD

1. Place the salad ingredients in a serving bowl.

2. Mix together the yogurt, horseradish and spices.

3. Toss the salad in the dressing.

Illustrated opposite

TOMATO ~ ORANGE SALAD
WITH NUTMEG DRESSING

INGREDIENTS

4 tomatoes
2 oranges
8oz (250g) broccoli
4oz (125g) turnip

DRESSING

juice and rind of ½ orange
1 tbsp (15ml) white wine vinegar
1 tbsp (15ml) sunflower oil
¼ tsp grated nutmeg
salt and pepper

•

NUTRITION PROFILE

*High in Vitamins A, C, E, calcium and
folic acid, this salad is also quite low in
calories.*

• Per portion •
Carbohydrate: 8.7g
Protein: 3.2g **Fibre:** 4.9g
Fat: 3.9g **Calories:** 80

*In this colourful salad, the turnip and broccoli create a solid base for the
Vitamin C-rich oranges and tomatoes. A hint of spice in the dressing
lends an added tang to the pervading orange flavour.*

Preparation time: 15 mins
Serves 4

METHOD

1. Slice the tomatoes. Peel and segment the oranges. Wash and
trim the broccoli. Scrub then chop the turnip.

2. For the dressing, mix the ingredients and season to taste.

3. Toss the dressing into the salad and serve immediately.

Illustrated opposite

Clockwise from top: **Tomato and orange salad with nutmeg dressing** (*see above*); **Fruit and fennel salad** (*see above*);
Californian salad with tarragon dressing (*see p.61*).

GREEN AND WHITE SALAD
WITH TOFU AND ANISEED DRESSING

INGREDIENTS

4oz (125g) mild onion
2oz (50g) mung bean sprouts (see p.29)
2oz (50g) shelled fresh peas
½ cucumber, diced
2oz (50g) pumpkin seeds

DRESSING
½ × 10oz (300g) packet silken tofu
1 tbsp (15ml) sesame oil
1 tbsp (15ml) cider vinegar
½ tsp aniseed

•

NUTRITION PROFILE

*This high-protein dish is a good source of
calcium, copper and Vitamins C and E.*

• Per portion •
Carbohydrate: 6.8g
Protein: 6.6g   **Fibre:** 1.9g
Fat: 10.7g   **Calories:** 150

*Crunchy salads are fun to eat, but can be easier to digest when mixed
with a smooth dressing. The pumpkin seeds, peas and mung beans
contain a wide range of vitamins and minerals and supplement the
protein provided by the tofu in the dressing.*

Preparation time: 15 mins
Serves 4

METHOD

1. Peel and chop the onion and rinse the mung bean sprouts.

2. Mix all the salad ingredients together in a large bowl.

3. For the dressing, mix the ingredients. Toss into the salad and
serve immediately.

Illustrated opposite

FLORENCE SALAD

INGREDIENTS

2 fennel bulbs
2 pears, preferably William or Packham
2oz (50g) unsalted peanuts
4oz (125g) young spinach leaves

DRESSING
3oz (75g) cottage cheese
1 tbsp (15ml) lemon juice
1 tbsp (15ml) smetana
2 tbsp (30ml) mayonnaise (see p.66)
½ tsp celery seeds
salt and pepper

•

NUTRITION PROFILE

*A highly nutritious recipe, this salad is high
in protein, fibre, Vitamins A, C and E and
in folic acid and calcium.*

• Per portion •
Carbohydrate: 11.8g
Protein: 10.7g   **Fibre:** 10.1g
Fat: 13.3g   **Calories:** 210

*This light, crisp salad has a deliciously rich, creamy dressing. If you
want to reduce the calories, use a low-calorie mayonnaise or add only a
little dressing to the salad and pass round the rest in a separate bowl.*

Preparation time: 20 mins
Serves 4

METHOD

1. Trim the fennel bulbs, slice in half and remove the centre
layers, leaving a shell for serving the salad. Cut the centre layers
into coarse chunks.

2. Core and chop the pears and mix with the fennel and peanuts.
Select the best spinach leaves and rinse.

3. For the dressing, mix all the ingredients together in a blender
or food processor until completely smooth. Season to taste.

4. Mix the dressing into the salad.

5. Lay the spinach leaves on a large plate, pile the salad into the
fennel shell halves and lay them on top of the spinach base.

Illustrated opposite

Clockwise from top: **Red, white and green salad** (*see p.66*); **Florence salad** (*see above*);
Green and white salad with tofu and aniseed dressing (*see above*).

RED, WHITE AND GREEN SALAD

INGREDIENTS

1 red pepper, deseeded and diced
4oz (125g) mooli, scrubbed and diced
6oz (175g) mangetout, halved
4oz (125g) Chinese leaves, shredded

DRESSING

1 tbsp (15ml) sesame oil
1 tsp (5ml) shoyu
1 tsp (5ml) lemon juice
½ tsp honey
1 tsp (5ml) tahini

•

NUTRITION PROFILE

High in magnesium, this low-calorie salad is also a rich source of Vitamins A, C and E.

• Per portion •
Carbohydrate: 6.7g
Protein: 3.2g **Fibre:** 1.9g
Fat: 4.6g **Calories:** 85

This salad is excellent value as very little is wasted in the preparation of all the salad vegetables. Mooli, otherwise known as Daikon, is a large white radish, slightly milder in flavour than the traditional red skinned variety and with mangetout you eat everything as the name suggests. The sweet-and-sour dressing brings an appropriately oriental flavour to the Chinese-style salad.

Preparation time: 25 mins
Serves 4

METHOD

1. Prepare all the salad ingredients, and place in a salad bowl.

2. For the dressing, mix the ingredients thoroughly together.

3. Pour the dressing over the salad and toss.

Illustrated on page 65

CLASSIC MAYONNAISE

INGREDIENTS

2 egg yolks
½ pint (300ml) mixed olive and sunflower oil
1–2 tbsp (15–30ml) lemon juice or white wine vinegar
pinch mustard powder
salt and pepper
1 tbsp (15ml) boiling water

•

NUTRITION PROFILE

This mayonnaise is rich in Vitamins B_{12}, D and E.

• Per tablespoon •
Carbohydrate: – –
Protein: 0.6g **Fibre:** – –
Fat: 14.5g **Calories:** 135

A classic mayonnaise can be used as a base for other salad dressings as part of a recipe, or simply as a rich dressing in its own right. It is high in fat, so use sparingly or mix with natural yogurt or low-fat fromage frais. It will keep for at least a week in a cool place.

Preparation time: 15 mins (plus chilling time)
Makes ½ pint (300ml)

METHOD

1. Beat the egg yolks thoroughly, in a blender or with a whisk.

2. Add half the oil, a drip at a time, beating continuously.

3. Add 1 tbsp (15ml) lemon juice or vinegar and the mustard powder. Beat well.

4. Add the remaining oil: a tablespoon at a time if whisking by hand; in a steady stream if using an electric whisk. Season.

5. Beat in the boiling water, to stabilize the mayonnaise. Refrigerate and serve chilled.

Illustrated on page 68

MAKING MAYONNAISE

Mayonnaise provides a texture and flavour that contrasts and complements many different kinds of salad. It can be varied and adapted by adding different herbs and spices, part-mixing with cottage cheese, yogurt or tofu, and you can make it more substantial by mixing in finely chopped vegetables such as cucumber, onion or tomato. Have all the ingredients at room temperature before starting to prepare mayonnaise.

1. Beat the egg yolks thoroughly with a whisk. You can use a blender, but the mayonnaise will be thinner.

2. Take ¼ pint (150ml) oil and add it to the eggs one drop at a time, while beating continuously.

3. Thin down the mixture with 1 tbsp (15ml) vinegar or lemon juice, add the mustard powder and beat well. Gradually add the remaining oil and finally beat in 1 tbsp (15ml) boiling water.

LIGHT MAYONNAISE

INGREDIENTS
1 egg
1–2 tbsp (15–30ml) lemon juice or white wine vinegar
½ pint (300ml) mixed olive and sunflower oil
pinch mustard powder
salt and pepper
1 tbsp (15ml) boiling water

•

NUTRITION PROFILE

This mayonnaise is rich in Vitamins E and D, contains B_{12} and is lower in cholesterol than the classic version.

• Per tablespoon •
Carbohydrate: – –
Protein: 0.3g   **Fibre:** – –
Fat: 13.6g   **Calories:** 125

This lighter version of the classic mayonnaise uses only one egg, which helps to keep the calorie and cholesterol levels down. Since the mixture is also less likely to curdle, it is easy to make in a blender or food processor. The egg white will help to thicken the mixture.

Preparation time: 15 mins
Makes ½ pint (300ml)

METHOD

1. Using a whisk or blender, beat the egg thoroughly with the lemon juice or vinegar.

2. Add the oil very gradually, beating continuously.

3. When smooth, add the mustard powder and season to taste.

4. Beat in the boiling water to stabilize the mayonnaise.

Illustrated on page 68

AIOLI

INGREDIENTS

1 egg
1–2 tbsp (15–30ml) lemon juice or
white wine vinegar
3–4 cloves garlic
½ pint (300ml) mixed olive and
sunflower oil
pinch mustard powder
salt and pepper
1 tbsp (15ml) boiling water

•

NUTRITION PROFILE

*Garlic mayonnaise is rich in Vitamins D
and E and contains Vitamin B_{12}.*

• Per tablespoon •
Carbohydrate: 0.5g
Protein: 0.4g **Fibre:** – –
Fat: 13.6g **Calories:** 125

*This classic garlic mayonnaise from France is based on the Light
Mayonnaise (see p. 67), but for a richer, darker dressing, you could
use the Classic Mayonnaise (see p. 66) and add the garlic before
dripping in the oil.*

Preparation time: 20 mins
Makes ½ pint (300ml)

METHOD

1. In a food processor or blender, beat the egg thoroughly with
the lemon juice or vinegar.

2. Crush the cloves of garlic and stir into the egg mixture.

3. Add the oil very gradually, beating continuously.

4. When smooth, add the mustard powder and season to taste.

5. Beat in the boiling water to stabilize the mayonnaise.

Illustrated opposite

HERB MAYONNAISE

INGREDIENTS

1 egg
1–2 tbsp (15–30ml) lemon juice or
white wine vinegar
5–6 tbsp (75–90ml) chopped fresh
tarragon
½ pint (300ml) mixed olive and
sunflower oil
pinch mustard powder
salt and pepper
1 tbsp (15ml) boiling water

•

NUTRITION PROFILE

*Herb mayonnaise is rich in Vitamins D
and E and contains Vitamin B_{12}.*

• Per tablespoon •
Carbohydrate: – –
Protein: 0.4g **Fibre:** 0.2g
Fat: 13.6g **Calories:** 125

*If you prefer the rich Classic Mayonnaise (see p. 66) to the light
version, simply add the herbs to two beaten eggs. Parsley and chives
also work well with mayonnaise.*

Preparation time: 20 mins
Makes ½ pint (300ml)

METHOD

1. Beat the egg thoroughly with the lemon juice or vinegar.

2. Stir in the chopped herbs.

3. Add the oil very slowly, beating continuously.

4. When smooth, add the mustard powder and season to taste.

5. Beat in the boiling water to stabilize the mayonnaise.

Illustrated opposite

Clockwise from top left: **Low calorie mayonnaise** (see p. 70); **Aioli** (see above); **Herb mayonnaise** (see above);
Curried mayonnaise (see p. 70); **Classic mayonnaise** (see p. 66); **Light mayonnaise** (see p. 67).

CURRIED MAYONNAISE

INGREDIENTS

1 quantity of Classic or Light
Mayonnaise (see pp.66, 67)
1 small Spanish onion
2oz (50g) dried apricots
2 tbsp (30ml) concentrated apple juice
or honey
1/2 tsp turmeric
pinch cayenne
1/2 tsp cumin seeds
1/2 tsp chopped fresh coriander leaves
salt and pepper
•

NUTRITION PROFILE

*Rich in Vitamins D and E, this dressing
also contains Vitamin B_{12}.*

• Per tablespoon •
Carbohydrate: 1.9g
Protein: 0.9g **Fibre:** 0.7g
Fat: 14.6g **Calories:** 140

*This spicy mayonnaise can be used as a rich dressing, dip or sauce. The
added ingredients contribute additional vitamins and minerals without
significantly adding to the calories. If you are anxious to reduce
calories, however, use the lighter version as a base.*

Preparation time: 30 mins
Makes 1/2 pint (300ml)

METHOD

1. Make up the mayonnaise, using the light or classic method.

2. Peel the onion and dice finely.

3. Cut the dried apricots into small pieces.

4. Mix the onion, apricots, concentrated apple juice and spices
into the mayonnaise.

5. Season to taste.

Illustrated on page 68

LOW-CALORIE MAYONNAISE

INGREDIENTS

1/4 pint (150ml) Light Mayonnaise
1/4 pint (150ml) natural yogurt
1/2 red pepper
1 tsp (5ml) paprika
salt and pepper
•

NUTRITION PROFILE

*Much lower in fat and calories than
traditional mayonnaise, this dressing also
contains calcium and Vitamins B_{12}, C,
D and E.*

• Per tablespoon •
Carbohydrate: 0.5g
Protein: 0.6g **Fibre:** – –
Fat: 6.9g **Calories:** 65

*This low-fat mayonnaise, made half of mayonnaise and half of yogurt
is enriched by the added spice and red pepper and makes a good creamy
dressing on any salad.*

Preparation time: 10 mins (plus 15 mins if making mayonnaise)
Makes 1/2 pint (300ml)

METHOD

1. Mix together the mayonnaise and yogurt.

2. Deseed the red pepper and dice finely.

3. Add the pepper and paprika to the dressing.

4. Season to taste.

Illustrated on page 68

From top: **Peanut and tomato dressing** (*see p.73*); **Walnut dressing** (*see p.74*);
Chinese dressing (*see p.73*); **Cider dressing** (*see p.74*); **French dressing** (*see p.72*).

FRENCH DRESSING

INGREDIENTS

1 tbsp (15ml) white wine vinegar
4 tbsp (60ml) olive oil
2 spring onions, trimmed and finely chopped
1–2 cloves garlic, crushed
salt and pepper

•

NUTRITION PROFILE

French dressing contains a small amount of Vitamin E.

• Per tablespoon •
Carbohydrate: 0.8g
Protein: 0.1g   **Fibre:** 0.1g
Fat: 10.8g   **Calories:** 100

A versatile oil and vinegar dressing has countless possibilities for variations with herbs and spices. This is a slightly lighter and sharper version of a recipe much favoured on the Continent of 1 part vinegar to 6 parts oil, but milder than the traditional 1 to 3 ratio.

Preparation time: 10 mins
Makes 3 fl oz (75ml)

METHOD

1. Mix together all the ingredients very thoroughly. Season to taste, and store in a screw-topped jar in the fridge.

2. Shake vigorously before using. If you make larger quantities, it will keep for at least 2 weeks if refrigerated.

Illustrated on page 71

MAKING FRENCH DRESSING

French dressing, also known as vinaigrette, is a general term for a multitude of variations. Bearing in mind the kind of salad you are dressing, you can experiment by using different oils (seed, nut or bean) for the base, or different combinations of herbs and spices for the seasoning.

1. Pour the vinegar into a large, screw-topped jam jar and add the onions and garlic. Leave for the flavours to mix.

2. Slowly stir in the oil and mix thoroughly. Season to taste.

3. Screw the lid firmly on the jar and shake vigorously before using.

PEANUT AND TOMATO DRESSING

INGREDIENTS

1oz (25g) salted peanuts
2 tomatoes, skinned and chopped
1 tsp (5ml) tomato purée
2–3 tbsp (10–15ml) lemon juice
3 tbsp (45ml) peanut or groundnut oil
pinch chilli powder
salt and pepper

•

NUTRITION PROFILE

This dressing is rich in Vitamins C and E and contains zinc.

• Per tablespoon •
Carbohydrate: 0.4g
Protein: 0.04g **Fibre:** 0.3g
Fat: 2.9g **Calories:** 40

This tangy, colourful dressing adds interest to the simplest green salad and contributes a healthy quantity of protein and Vitamin C.

Preparation time: 15 mins
Makes 7 fl oz (200ml)

METHOD

1. In a food processor, grind the peanuts into fine pieces.

2. Add the tomatoes, purée and lemon juice and blend thoroughly.

3. Gradually drip in the oil, blending continuously, until the mixture is thick and creamy.

4. Add the chilli powder and season to taste.

Illustrated on page 71

CHINESE DRESSING

INGREDIENTS

½ green chilli
1 clove garlic
1 tbsp (15ml) sunflower oil
1 tsp (5ml) sesame oil
1 tbsp (15ml) cider vinegar
1 tsp (5ml) shoyu
1 tsp (5ml) sherry
1 tsp (5ml) gomashio (sesame salt)

•

NUTRITION PROFILE

Low in calories and fat, this dressing is a good source of Vitamin E.

• Per tablespoon •
Carbohydrate: 1.5g
Protein: 0.1g **Fibre:** – –
Fat: 4.5g **Calories:** 50

This sharp, spicy dressing mixes well with strong-flavoured vegetables, beansprouts and tofu. To make your own gomashio, grind 5–10 parts roasted sesame seeds with 1 part salt.

Preparation time: 15 mins
Makes 2 fl oz (60ml)

METHOD

1. Deseed and dice the chilli. Crush the garlic.

2. Mix all the ingredients together, stirring thoroughly.

3. Store in a screw-topped jar in the fridge and shake well before using. If you make larger quantities, it will keep for about 2 weeks.

Illustrated on page 71

WALNUT DRESSING

INGREDIENTS

4oz (125g) walnut pieces
2 cloves garlic
1/2–1 tsp (2–5ml) green peppercorns
1 tsp (5ml) miso
2 tbsp (30ml) olive oil
2 tbsp (30ml) lemon juice
2 fl oz–1/4 pint (50–150ml) water

•

NUTRITION PROFILE

*This recipe contains small amounts of
magnesium and zinc.*

• Per tablespoon •
Carbohydrate: 0.6g
Protein: 0.7g   **Fibre:** 0.3g
Fat: 4.6g   **Calories:** 45

*This substantial dressing goes well with chunky salads, beansprouts or
savoury rissoles. To prevent the mixture curdling, add the water very
slowly while you blend. This allows it to emulsify with the oils in the
nuts without separating.*

Preparation time: 10 mins
Makes 1/2 pint (300ml)

METHOD

1. In a food processor, grind the walnuts with the garlic and
peppercorns.

2. Add the miso, olive oil and lemon juice and blend.

3. Add the water very gradually, blending continuously, until the
dressing has the consistency of thick yogurt.

Illustrated on page 71

CIDER DRESSING

INGREDIENTS

6 tbsp (90ml) sweet cider
juice of 1 lemon
2 tbsp (30ml) sunflower oil
2 tsp (10ml) concentrated apple juice
1/4 tsp ground allspice
1/4 tsp grated nutmeg

•

NUTRITION PROFILE

*This low-calorie dressing is a good source
of Vitamin E.*

• Per tablespoon •
Carbohydrate: 0.3g
Protein: – –   **Fibre:** – –
Fat: 1.5g   **Calories:** 15

*Cider and concentrated apple juice give a fruity flavour and help to
reduce the sharp flavour left by cutting down on oil. The spices add zest
without acidity.*

Preparation time: 10 mins
Makes 1/4 pint (150ml)

METHOD

1. Mix all the ingredients together thoroughly and store in a
screw-topped jar in the fridge. It will keep for about 2 weeks.

2. Shake well before using.

Illustrated on page 71

DESERTS

The last course gives a chance to balance up
a meal. A fresh fruit salad after a filling
main course adds vitamins without extra
fat, while a rich carob pudding can be
nutritious and satisfying after a light meal.

HAZELNUT AND RASPBERRY DESSERT

INGREDIENTS

2oz (50g) medium oatmeal
½oz (15g) hazelnuts, ground
½ tsp ground allspice
½ pint (300ml) natural yogurt
1–2 tbsp (15–30ml) whisky
2 bananas
8oz (250g) raspberries

•

NUTRITION PROFILE

*High in fibre and low in fat, this dessert is a
good source of magnesium and Vitamins
B$_6$, C and E.*

• Per portion •
Carbohydrate: 27.3g
Protein: 6.5g **Fibre:** 7.4g
Fat: 2.9g **Calories:** 170

*This deliciously rich pudding is surprisingly healthy – low in fat and high
in fibre. The light toasting brings out the flavour of the grain and the
hint of hazelnuts adds much to the overall effect. Other soft fruits in
season will work equally well.*

Preparation time: 40 mins (plus chilling time)
Serves 4

METHOD

1. Mix the oatmeal and hazelnuts together and place on a baking
sheet. Roast in a preheated oven at Gas Mark 4, 350°F, 180°C for
8–10 minutes.

2. Add the allspice and allow to cool.

3. Mix the yogurt with the whisky.

4. Slice the bananas, and reserve 4 slices for garnish. Rinse the
raspberries.

5. Spoon layers of fruit, grain and yogurt into 4 individual glasses.
Finish with a layer of yogurt and garnish with a slice of banana.
Refrigerate and serve chilled.

Illustrated on page 77

AUTUMN FRUIT SALAD

INGREDIENTS

2 oranges
1 red apple
1 green apple
1 firm pear (preferably William or Packham)

TOPPING
5oz (150g) silken tofu
3 tbsp (45ml) lemon juice
1 tsp (5ml) concentrated apple juice
½ inch (2.5cm) fresh root ginger, peeled and grated

GARNISH
½oz (15g) pumpkin seeds

•

NUTRITION PROFILE

This fruit salad is a good source of Vitamin C, calcium and copper.

• Per portion •
Carbohydrate: 14.3g
Protein: 3.4g **Fibre:** 2.6g
Fat: 2.8g **Calories:** 95

The secret of a really good fruit salad is to use large chunks of firm fruit and to add plenty of citrus fruit to supply the moisture. Autumn fruits are inexpensive and a low-fat topping keeps the calories down. You can vary the dish by adding other fruits in season. If you select them carefully for their colour and texture, you can achieve a pleasing visual effect which will complement this light sweet.

Preparation time: 30 mins
Serves 4

METHOD

1. Peel the oranges. Divide into segments, allowing the juice to drip into a bowl.

2. Chop the apples and pear into chunks, removing the cores.

3. Mix with the orange segments and juice and refrigerate.

4. For the topping, blend the ingredients together in a blender or food processor until smooth.

5. Serve the fruit in individual bowls with a spoonful of topping and garnish with pumpkin seeds.

Illustrated opposite

Clockwise from top left: **Hazelnut and raspberry dessert** (*see p. 75*); **Pineapple basket** (*see p. 78*); **Autumn fruit salad** (*see above*).

PINEAPPLE BASKET

INGREDIENTS

2 small pineapples
6oz (175g) cantaloupe or honeydew
melon
1 mango
1 passion fruit
1oz (25g) fresh coconut, coarsely grated

TOPPING

1oz (25g) fresh coconut
½oz (15g) shelled walnuts

•

NUTRITION PROFILE

*This high-fibre dessert provides magnesium
and is rich in Vitamins A, B₁ and C.*

• Per portion •
Carbohydrate: 40.7g
Protein: 2.1g **Fibre:** 6.8g
Fat: 5.8g **Calories:** 220

*This exotic fruit salad makes a wonderfully festive and refreshing
dessert for a special occasion. Select the fruit carefully – you can
usually tell if it is ripe by the smell.*

Preparation time: 40 mins
Serves 4

METHOD

1. Slice the pineapples in half lengthways and scoop out the inner
flesh with a sharp knife.

2. Scoop out the melon flesh into small balls. Peel and slice the
mango. Scoop out the flesh of the passion fruit.

3. Mix all the fruit with the grated coconut.

4. Pile the fruit back into the pineapple shells or serve in bowls.

5. For the topping, grind the coconut and walnuts together in a
food processor or nut mill and sprinkle over the fruit.

6. If you like, grill for 2 minutes until just brown.

Illustrated on page 77

MAKING A PINEAPPLE CASE

*A scooped-out pineapple makes an attractive and exotic-looking case for a tropical-style fruit salad. As well
as the fresh colour and interesting shape, it makes a sturdy and generous container. Oranges and lemons also
make attractive cases, usually for sorbets and ice creams, and can be prepared in the same way as pineapple.
To harden the cases before filling, leave in the fridge overnight.*

1. Working from the leaf end, cut the
pineapple in half lengthways with a
sharp knife.

2. Score carefully around the sides with
a knife leaving a broad casing and scoop
out the flesh with a knife and spoon.

3. Alternatively, cut a lid off the
pineapple and scoop out the flesh in the
same way.

HUNZA APRICOTS WITH SWEET TAHINI CREAM

INGREDIENTS

10oz (300g) Hunza apricots
1 tsp (5ml) concentrated apple juice

TOPPING
2 tbsp (30ml) tahini
3–4 tbsp (45–60ml) water
3 drops vanilla essence
4 tbsp (60ml) natural yogurt
1 tsp (5ml) clear honey

•

NUTRITION PROFILE

Extremely high in fibre and low in fat, this dessert is a good source of iron, calcium, and magnesium, niacin and Vitamin A.

• Per portion •
Carbohydrate: 34.8g
Protein: 6.3g **Fibre:** 19.8g
Fat: 4.3g **Calories:** 195

Hunza or wild apricots are whole, sun-dried apricots that come complete with stone. When soaked and eaten raw, they have a sweet, subtle flavour. You can make fruit sauces from the soaking liquid, and a delicious sweetener from the stewing juice.

Preparation time: 10 mins (plus overnight soaking time)
Serves 4

METHOD

1. Wash the apricots and soak overnight in plenty of water. Next day, drain most of the juice and keep for fruit salads.

2. Add the concentrated apple juice to the moistened apricots.

3. For the topping, mix the tahini thoroughly with the water until smooth. Add the remaining ingredients and mix well.

4. Pour the cream over the apricots or serve separately. Garnish with shredded orange rind.

Illustrated on page 80

SPICED EASTERN FRUITS

INGREDIENTS

3oz (75g) dried apricots
3oz (75g) dried peaches
2oz (50g) dried figs
2oz (50g) sultanas
2 sachets rosehip and hibiscus tea
6 cloves
6 cardamom seeds

GARNISH
1/2oz (15g) sliced pistachio nuts

•

NUTRITION PROFILE

A high-fibre recipe, this fruit salad is also rich in Vitamin A and iron.

• Per portion •
Carbohydrate: 16.4g
Protein: 1.4g **Fibre:** 3.4g
Fat: 0.7g **Calories:** 75

A compote of dried fruit makes a wonderful staple dish, always on hand and constantly being replenished. Dried fruits are a very concentrated form of goodness, so use sparingly. Soaking the fruit brings out the flavour, and gives the best value for money.

Preparation time: 20 mins (plus 2–3 days soaking time)
Serves 8

METHOD

1. Chop the apricots and peaches into fine slivers.

2. Remove the hard stalk of the figs, and dice them finely.

3. Mix all the fruits together.

4. Pour 1 1/2 pints (900ml) boiling water over the fruit and add the sachets of tea, cloves and cardamom.

5. Leave covered in the fridge for at least 2 days, adding a little more water if necessary.

6. To serve, remove the spices and garnish with sliced pistachio nuts.

Illustrated on page 80

FRUIT ~ OAT FREEZE

INGREDIENTS

2oz (50g) mixed nuts
6oz (175g) fresh fruit (strawberries,
apples, pears, oranges)
1 banana
4oz (125g) porridge oats
1 tbsp (15ml) wheatgerm
2oz (50g) raisins
2 tbsp (30ml) concentrated apple juice
1 tsp (5 ml) ground cinnamon
4–6 drops almond essence

•

NUTRITION PROFILE

*Rich in Vitamins B_1, C and E,
magnesium and iron, this dessert is also
high in fibre and protein.*

• Per portion •
Carbohydrate: 47.2g
Protein: 8.5g **Fibre:** 6.9g
Fat: 9.3g **Calories:** 305

*A cross between a pudding and a cake, this high-fibre, protein-rich
mixture makes a filling dessert after a salad. Whether you eat it as a
snack or as a dessert, try to keep the pieces small.*

Preparation time: 45 mins (plus 2 hours freezing time)
Serves 4

METHOD

1. In a food processor or nut mill, grind the nuts quite finely.

2. Reserve 2 strawberries for the garnish, then purée the banana
and fresh fruit in a blender or food processor.

3. Mix the nuts and fruit with the remaining ingredients, until
the mixture is moist but not sloppy. Add more oats if necessary.

4. Spoon the mixture into a 1 lb (500g) loaf tin, lined with
greaseproof paper, and freeze for about 2 hours.

5. Turn out and serve in small pieces garnished with strawberries.

Illustrated on page 83

FRESH CHERRY PASHKA

INGREDIENTS

4oz (125g) curd cheese
6 tbsp (90ml) natural yogurt
1oz (25g) polyunsaturated margarine
1 tbsp (15ml) raisins or sultanas
2 tsp (10ml) chopped nuts
3oz (75g) stoned cherries

•

NUTRITION PROFILE

*This low-calorie dessert is rich in Vitamin
D and calcium and contains a small
amount of Vitamin B_{12}.*

• Per portion •
Carbohydrate: 4.4g
Protein: 5.1g **Fibre:** 0.6g
Fat: 12g **Calories:** 145

*This is a healthy lower-fat adaptation of a traditional Russian Easter
pudding. It is easy to make, looks good and will keep for about 2–3
days. For an attractive garnish, add a whole walnut, a sprig of mint
and some chopped nuts.*

Preparation time: 20 mins (plus 12 hours standing time)
Serves 4

METHOD

1. Mix together the curd cheese and yogurt.

2. Beat in the margarine with a whisk.

3. Stir in the dried fruit and chopped nuts. Halve the cherries and
mix in gently.

4. Pierce an 8oz (250g) carton or use a flower pot, line with
muslin and stand on a plate. Spoon in the pashka. Cover and
weigh down. Leave to stand for 12 hours.

5. Turn out and unwrap. Serve in small slices.

Illustrated on page 83

Bottom: **Hunza apricots with sweet tahini cream** (*see p.79*); Top: **Spiced eastern fruits** (*see p.79*).

CASHEW AND CAROB PUDDING

INGREDIENTS

4oz (125g) cashew nuts
6 cardamom pods
4oz (125g) cottage cheese
1 tbsp (15ml) carob powder
1 ripe banana, peeled
2 tbsp (30ml) rum
up to 4 fl oz (125ml) water

GARNISH
banana slices
chopped cashews

•

NUTRITION PROFILE

This high-protein dessert is a good source of magnesium and Vitamin B_1.

• Per portion •
Carbohydrate: 15.5g
Protein: 10g   **Fibre:** 5.6g
Fat: 15.7g   **Calories:** 245

This makes a superbly rich, mousse-like pudding. Carob powder is a healthy alternative to cocoa. It is sweeter than cocoa and has a lower fat content. The addition of water and cottage cheese also helps to keep the fat content down. The combination of banana, rum, and carob powder creates a distinctly Caribbean flavour.

Preparation time: 15 mins
Serves 4

METHOD

1. In a food processor, grind the cashew nuts thoroughly with the cardamom pods.

2. Add the cottage cheese, carob powder, banana and rum. Then blend until completely smooth.

3. Gradually add the water until the mixture has the consistency of thick yogurt.

4. Spoon the mixture into individual glasses and garnish with banana and cashews. Serve immediately.

Illustrated opposite

Clockwise from top: **Fruit and oat freeze** (*see p.81*); **Cashew and carob pudding** (*see above*); **Fresh cherry pashka** (*see p.81*).